WORT...SATZ...GESPRÄCH

Beginning German Communication

RAINER SELL
UNIVERSITY OF MICHIGAN
DEARBORN

D1709618

Heinle & Heinle Publishers, Inc.
Boston, Massachusetts 02210 U.S.A.

Cover and Text Design: **Judy Poe**
Art Direction: **Len Shalansky**
Production: **Traute M. Marshall**

We wish to thank the following for providing us with photographs:
Uta Hoffmann 3, 90, 120   Rainer Sell 4   German Information Service 5, 54, 65,
73, 162, 164, 191, 193, 195, 226   Judy Poe 8, 194   Ernst Haas Studio 9   Cour-
tesy O.K.Harris Works of Art, New York 11   Herlinde Koelbl/Kay Reese & Associ-
ates 19   UPI Bettmann Archive 43, 158   J.H.Darchinger/Econ-Verlag 44   IN-
Press/dpa 52   Peter Southwick/Stock Boston 113   Elizabeth Crews/Stock Boston
123   Peter Menzel/Stock Boston 125, 177, 224   Michael Weisbrot/Stock Boston
135   Judy S. Gelles/Stock Boston 137   Ellis Herwig/Stock Boston 156, 225
Owen Franken/Stock Boston 227

Manufactured in the United States of America.
ISBN 0-8384-1293-9

Für Donna, Julian und Claudia

INHALTSVERZEICHNIS

Preface

Rationale and Method:

Wort—Satz—Gespräch is a communication reader for the first year of German. It can be used as a supplementary text with any beginning German program (typically as early as the fourth or fifth week of instruction) or as the main text for any beginning German Communication/Conversation course. Communication by free association of words and ideas is the underlying principle of the book. A variety of textual and pictorial cues stimulate the development of independent communication skills right from the start by allowing students to choose their own linguistic means and level of communication. They can communicate as often and as much as they are able, as soon as they are able. The topics and communication activities were all chosen with the same goal—to allow and encourage students to tap their own personal experiences, feelings, and imagination, as well as their environment in order to communicate spontaneously and effectively in German. By showing students the process by which we can learn to speak another language and by guiding them through this process step-by-step, we hope to develop self-motivated, independent language learners.

Topics and Activities:

Since spontaneous communication depends on students having something to say and being eager to say it, the topics and activities focus on the shared experiences and shared interests of today's students: John Travolta and his films, Superman, Muhammed Ali, prejudice, daily routines, friends, family, pets, cartoons, a projected Playboy club, to cite just a few themes. The activities are extensions of the main text. They do not follow a strict pattern and are designed to allow students maximum freedom in deciding what they want to say and how they will say it. The humorous tone of many of the activities should encourage students to enjoy the lighter side of language learning. After all, communicating in a new language is playing with words, and play should be fun.

Grammar:

The book is truly geared toward the first year of German by progressing in step with the weekly grammar assignments of most Beginning German texts. The grammatical focus of each chapter is indicated under "Grammar" in the table of contents and is briefly surveyed at the end of the chapter. The texts use simple structures appropriate for beginning communication in German. The frequent use of important simple structures will help students gain confidence in their communicative skills and internalize the essentials of grammar and syntax.

Built-in Workbook:

The book is designed as a combined communication reader and workbook so that students experience their preparation for class as an integral part of their personal progress in the language and as meaningful "personal property." Suggested activities can be done orally in class or, in many cases, as written preparation for oral communication. Instructors should make sure that final written entries are correct.

Photographs and Drawings:

Many photographs and drawings are integrated into the text through questions and other references. Their purpose goes beyond mere illustration. They are intended as visual cues that will trigger a variety of associations and responses far beyond what pictures and texts show. Communication about the "Supermarket Lady" in Chapter 2, for instance, need not be exhausted by mentioning her curlers, weight, shopping cart etc. but could include comments on supermarkets, shopping, Americans, health, sickness, sports, eating, drinking, personal likes, dislikes etc.

Vocabulary and Glosses:

The emphasis in this text is on using basic and already familiar vocabulary in different situations rather than on introducing new vocabulary in systematic fashion. Students are encouraged to use any vocabulary they know from other sources. In this way they will gain mastery of a limited, but essential vocabulary and develop confidence in their ability to communicate in German. Words that are not listed in Pfeffer's *Grunddeutsch* are glossed in the margins. There is an end vocabulary for all German words used in the book, and a limited English-German glossary to assist in the preparation of activities.

Acknowledgments

I would like to thank Charles H. Heinle and Stanley J. Galek of Heinle & Heinle for being open to a new approach to teaching communication in a foreign language; Walter Josef Denk of Lansing Community College for evaluating critically the manuscript in its early stages; Phillip J. Campana of Tennessee Technological University, Gerhard P. Knapp of the University of Utah, and Claire J. Kramsch of Massachusetts Institute of Technology for their constructive criticism of the manuscript and support of the project; my wife Donna-Christine for her inspiration, critical feed-back, and expert typing of the manuscript; Susan Troost of Detroit for painstakingly composing both glossaries; Judy Poe for the attractive cover and design of the book; Len Shalansky for providing humorous illustrations that underscore the spirit of the book; and Traute M. Marshall of Heinle & Heinle for her excellent advice and informed editing, and for reading my mind when choosing many of the photographs.

Rainer Sell

WORT...SATZ...GESPRÄCH

KAPITEL 1

Rose...
Rot...
Ich liebe dich

Have you ever noticed how one word can trigger another word, or a sentence fragment, or a whole sentence sometimes? Often, the connection is not achieved through logic but is brought about by *association*, a much more open-ended and flexible mechanism. In fact, our consciousness is rife with such loose, "disorderly" associations quite apart from the logic with which we have been trained to speak and write.

Why not make use of the freedom and richness of association to communicate in German? With even a rudimentary knowledge of German, everybody can participate—at his or her own pace and level of competence. Nobody need be put on the spot, yet everybody has to follow the associative chain of communication in order to understand and contribute. The associative units should be kept short (one sentence at most), and the exchange should be brisk and unstructured. Start with any word, continue an associative exchange as long as it flows; then pick a new word.

ASSOCIATIVE CHAINS AND WORD FIELDS

A LOOK AT SOME ASSOCIATIVE CHAINS that might develop from the word „gelb."

1. Sonne...Sand...Ferien...am Strand°...es ist heiß...Eis°...
2. braun...weiß...schwarz...grün...das Gras ist grün...
3. Banane...Dschungel...ich habe Angst...Tarzan...Tiger...
4. Farbe...Maler°...van Gogh...van Gogh ist tot°...wir leben...wir leben gut...Auto und Haus und Kühlschrank...das ist materialistisch...kommunistisch...sind Sie Kommunist?...nein! sind Sie Faschist?...ich bin Student...ich auch...kein Geld... arm...der Professor ist reich...ein Kapitalist...Kapitalismus...

beach
ice, ice cream

painter
dead

Sequence 2 exhibits a specialized, rational use of the associative technique. You will soon run out of words if you continue this way. Hopefully somebody will break out of this "system" and give the sequence a different, truly open direction. If not, you can start with a new word. Do the same if the sequence becomes too much like traditional conversation or fails to include the whole group. Go back to one-word associations.

Sequence 2 in our example, the collection of colors, represents a special form of the associative sequence: the word field. Producing word fields is a more systematic, but still playful activity that allows you to review effectively what you know in a given field or to pursue what you might want to know. The more rationally inclined among you might want to subdivide the word field into nouns, adjectives, and verbs.

EXAMPLE:

s Auto	fahren	schnell	
s Benzin	tanken°	schmutzig	to gas up
e Tankstelle°	halten	modern	filling station
s Öl	kaufen	leer	
e Batterie	starten	kaputt°	broken
e Kupplung°	schalten°	defekt	clutch
e Bremsen (pl)°	bremsen°	heiß	to shift (gears)
r Kühler°	kühlen°	groß	brakes
r Kofferraum°	öffnen°		to brake
	anhalten		radiator (of car)
	abbiegen		to cool
			trunk (of car)
			to open

3

B **DEVELOP ASSOCIATIVE SEQUENCES** in class or write down your own personal associative sequence using the following words as starters. Produce at least 15 associative units.

1. Auto   2. Bier   3. schlafen   4. krank   5. Politik

C **PRODUCE WORD FIELDS** for the following words (at least 15 words per field).

studieren

das Haus

die Ferien

E **RECOUNT YOUR DAY BY ASSOCIATION.**

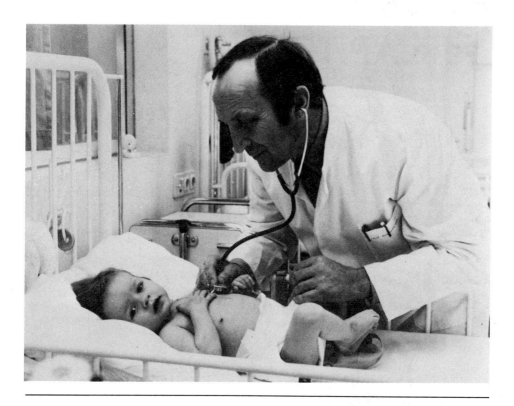

D LOOK AT THE PICTURES. Treat them as visual cues that trigger associative
chains. Do not limit yourself to enumerations or descriptions of what you see,
but rather speculate boldly about: who and what is there, what people are doing or
not doing, why they are there, where they come from, what they think, say, and wish,
which time of the day or what season it is, the weather, temperature, sizes and
shapes of people, numbers, relationships, colors, generalizations about people, activities, location, bold comparisons and identifications (,,Das ist Onkel Hans. Er ist
dick.''), expectations and subjective judgements (good, bad, intelligent, stupid, etc.).

 Many German jokes depend on regionalism. The inhabitants of a specific area are singled out by the rest of Germany for their alleged characteristics and weaknesses. One of the more recent victims in this respect
have been the ,,Ostfriesen'' (East Frisians), the inhabitants of a relatively
remote agricultural area bordering the North Sea. Unjustly, of course,
they have been stereotyped as being very slow thinkers, very slow speakers, and
generally a little dense. After reading the following joke, you will be convinced that
your associative powers far exceed those of the ,,Ostfriesen.''

Der Ostfriese Hanno trifft° den Ostfriesen Heino.   *meets*
Hanno sagt: ,,Na?''°   *well (colloquial)*
Da sagt Heino: ,,Na, und?''

KAPITEL 2

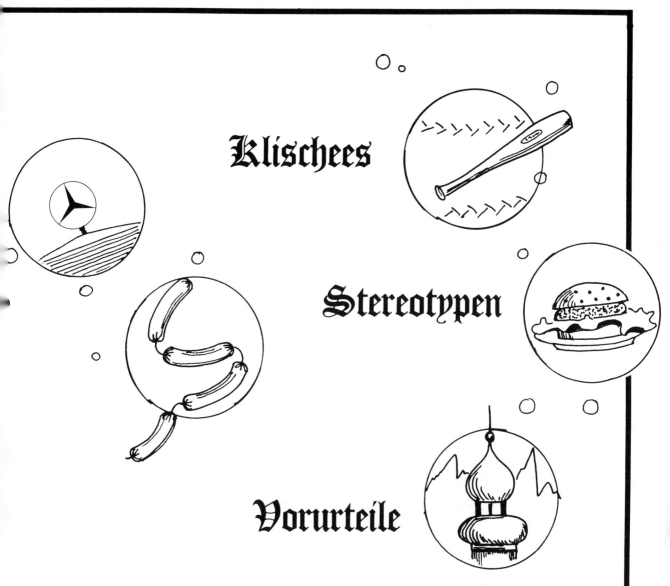

Klischees

Stereotypen

Vorurteile

We all use stereotypes from time to time to refer to this or that group of people. Although we are aware of the falseness and potential danger of stereotyping, we often indulge in it as a quick way of passing judgement. One way to deal with prejudices, stereotypes, and clichés is to indulge in them intentionally and carry them to their ridiculous extremes. It is in this spirit that you should approach Kapitel 2: as fun and as therapy.

DIE DEUTSCHEN UND DIE AMERIKANER

Die Deutschen:

emperor
protect
leather shorts or
pants

Die Deutschen sind fleißig.
Sie sind dick.
Die Deutschen haben viel Geld.
Sie haben keinen Humor.
Die Deutschen trinken immer Bier.
Sie essen nur Sauerkraut.
Sie singen laut.
Sie wandern immer.

Die Deutschen lieben Musik.
Die Deutschen brauchen einen Kaiser.°
Sie schützen° die Natur.
Die Deutschen tragen alle Lederhosen.°
Sie machen immer Ferien.
Sie fahren alle einen Mercedes.
Die Deutschen heißen alle Fritz.

Was tragen die Männer? Warum blasen sie? Wie ist das Wetter? Warum sehen wir keine Frauen? Ich finde die Männer ... Warum? Ich finde das Bild ... Warum?

A WAS SAGEN UND DENKEN die drei Männer und der Hund?

Der Mann rechts sagt:

Der Mann links antwortet:

answers

Der Mann in der Mitte denkt:

in the middle

Der Hund denkt:

B Let us assume the men in the picture are married and their wives would be watching them on something like "Candid Camera:" **WHAT WOULD THE WOMEN SAY?**

Männer _____ .

_____ .

_____ .

C **THE FAT MAN IN THE MIDDLE TELLS US** why he cannot lose weight, how other people treat him, why he has a little dog, what he does for a living, etc.

_____

_____

_____

Die Amerikaner:

	Die Amerikaner sind optimistisch.
	Sie sind naiv.
	Die Amerikaner haben viel Geld.
taste	Die Amerikaner haben keinen Geschmack.°
	Sie trinken immer Coca-Cola.
	Sie essen nur Steak.
chewing gum	Die Amerikaner kauen immer Kaugummi.°
walk	Die Amerikaner gehen nie zu Fuß.°
	Die Amerikaner lieben Hamburger.
	Die Amerikanerinnen kochen nie.
protect rockets	Die Amerikaner schützen° Westeuropa mit Raketen.°
curlers	Die Amerikanerinnen tragen immer Lockenwickler.°
	Die Amerikaner machen alles aus Plastik.
own	Die Amerikaner besitzen° alle drei Cadillacs.
	Die Amerikaner heißen alle Joe.

A **WHAT CAN YOU SAY ABOUT THE "SUPERMARKET LADY?"** Expect your statement to be contradicted or negated. The English cues are meant to be suggestions, they are not mandatory.

Supermarket Lady
by Duane Hanson

Die Frau ist _____
(fat, heavy, young, old, maybe forty, a housewife, in the supermarket, typically American, typically German, sick, very healthy, a mother, optimistic, beautiful, married, not happy, lazy, friendly, a smoker, a student, rich, hungry, a filmstar, a feminist, etc.)

Die Frau hat _____
(a cigarette, curlers, a pullover, a handbag, much money, no money, a husband, children, a dog, much time, no taste, problems, friends, a car, etc.)

Die Frau _____
(smokes, buys a lot, drinks Coca-Cola, beer, always eats, does not play tennis, does not cook, studies every day, stays mostly at home, never dances, sings well, plays cards, loves chewing gum etc.)

B **INVENT A STORY** around the "Supermarket Lady: give her a family (or not), talk about her hobbies, likes, dislikes, her house, work, friends, problems etc.

C **PROVOKE YOUR CLASSMATES** with your own clichés and stereotypes of Germans and Americans. The following lists may provide some material.

Die Deutschen sind ...
Die Amerikaner sind ...
Die Amerikanerinnen sind ...

timid

Die Deutschen ...
Die Amerikaner ...
Die Amerikanerinnen ...

haben essen trinken brauchen lieben tragen kochen machen kein,-e,-en

rockets
Black Forest cherry cake

corn (maize)

too much

immer nur alle nur immer Brot Wasser Pistolen Raketen° Wurst

Schwarzwälder Kirschtorte° Bermudashorts Whisky mit Soda Kartoffeln

vier Autos pro Familie 8 Wochen Ferien pro Jahr einmal pro Woche Mais°

Popcorn zuviel° Geld zuviel Freizeit oft Ferien Diät Wein

D **MAKE UP OTHER PRECONCEPTIONS,** existing or imagined, about the following nationalities (4 for each).

1. **r** Engländer, -   England   englisch
   e Engländerin, -nen
2. **r** Franzose, -n°   Frankreich   französisch   *Frenchman*
   e Französin, -nen
3. **r** Italiener, -   Italien   italienisch
   e Italienerin, -nen

E **COMPLETE THE ENTRIES** for the following nationalities, and add some of your own choice. (Consult a dictionary or your teacher, if in doubt.)

1. **r** Mexikaner   _____   _____

   e _____

2. **r** Chinese   _____   _____

   e _____

3. **r** Spanier, -   _____   _____

   e _____

4. **r** _____   _____   _____

   e _____

5. **r** _____   _____   _____

   e _____

F **ASK "WARUM?" QUESTIONS** about some of the clichés on Germans and Americans and try to give explanations. Since we are dealing with prejudice, your explanation can be as phantastic and farfetched as the prejudice itself.

EXAMPLES: Warum sind die Deutschen dick?
Die Deutschen finden das schön.
Die Deutschen essen nur Kartoffeln.
Die Deutschen sitzen gern zu Hause.

discuss
Sie sitzen immer und diskutieren.°

Warum kochen die Amerikanerinnen nie?

too much
Die Amerikanerinnen studieren zuviel.°
Die Amerikanerinnen sind emanzipiert.
Die Familie geht zu McDonalds.
Sie arbeiten nur für Geld.
Sie telefonieren immer.

Warum trinken die Amerikaner nur Coca-Cola?

_____

_____

_____

G **TALK ABOUT THE POSSIBLE CONSEQUENCES** of such behavior or condition in a realistic or a fanciful way.

result
EXAMPLE: Die Deutschen sind dick. Was ist das Resultat?°
Sie sind zu schwer.
Sie laufen zu langsam.
Sie gehen oft zum Arzt.
Sie bleiben meistens zu Haus.
Der Arzt sagt: „Kein Bier—nur Wasser!"

Die Amerikanerinnen kochen nie. Was ist das Resultat?

H **STATE THE COMMON WISDOM** about an item.

chewing gum
better than
EXAMPLE: Kaugummi° ist zu süß.
besser als° Zahnpasta.
schlecht für die Zähne.
typisch amerikanisch.
nicht gesund.

Kaugummi hat zuviel Zucker.
keine Vitamine
auch Freunde in Deutschland.

Kaugummi kostet nicht viel.
        ärgert° die Lehrer.   *annoys*
        klebt überall.
        kommt aus Amerika.
        macht Kinder glücklich.

I   **COME UP WITH SIMILAR STATEMENTS** about *Sauerkraut, Plastik,* and *Bier.*

> Sauerkraut ist
>
> Sauerkraut hat
>
> Sauerkraut kostet
> Sauerkraut schmeckt

J   **WHAT DO YOU LIKE TO EAT? WHAT DO YOU LIKE TO DRINK?**

EXAMPLE: Ich esse gern Käse.
            Ich trinke gern Coca-Cola.

K   **NAME THINGS** that are made from these materials.

Der Tisch ist   aus Holz.
_____ aus Eisen.
_____ aus Gold.
_____ aus Glas.
_____ aus Silber.
_____ aus Plastik.
_____ aus Aluminium.
_____ aus Gummi.
_____
_____

INSTANT SUCCESS IN VOCABULARY BUILDING

the socialist   **r Sozialist, -en**

✱ **NOTE:** The stress is on the last syllable of the German singular. This is characteristic of many German nouns derived from Greek or Latin. Here is an excellent source of "easy" vocabulary: the words have usually the same meaning in German, the plural is always -en. The letter c changes to k or z according to the English pronunciation.

A FILL IN THE GERMAN EQUIVALENTS

the democrat	**r** Demokrat, -en
the terrorist	**r** Terrorist, -en
the pacifist	r _____
the student	_____
the president	_____ ä _____
the communist	_____
the capitalist	_____
the idiot	_____
the anarchist	_____

B USE THE NEW WORDS FOR NAME-CALLING

EXAMPLE: Du Kapitalist!   Du hast einen Mercedes.

_____ !   _____ .

_____ !   _____ .

_____ !   _____ .

C FIND THE ANTONYM

dick	_____	optimistisch	_____
uneducated gut	_____	ungebildet°	_____

reich	_____	viel	_____
fleißig	_____	interessant	_____
laut	_____		

D **USE THE ADJECTIVES IN SENTENCES** dealing with well-known public personalities.

ANGSTHASEN°

timid persons ("chickens")

One form of prejudice is fear of the outside world carried to the extreme. Very fearful people imagine everything that could happen to them, think it is bound to happen, and therefore become exceedingly cautious. This is a possible result:

Angsthasen fahren nicht nach New York.
Angsthasen fliegen nicht nach Europa.
Sie gehen nicht über die Straße.
Sie bleiben immer zu Haus.
Sie spielen nie Tennis.

	Sie tanzen nie.
most of the time	Angsthasen schlafen meistens.°
	Sie rauchen eine Zigarette pro Jahr.
	Sie trinken ein Glas Wein pro Jahr.
	Sie essen nur Hamburger.
	Sie haben keinen Hund.
	Sie kaufen einen Hund aus Plastik.
	Sie lesen die Zeitung von A bis Z.
the whole day	Sie hören den ganzen Tag° Radio.
account	Angsthasen haben ein Konto° in Zürich.
	Sie heiraten nicht.
	Angsthasen haben keine Kinder.
	Angsthasen gehen oft zum Arzt.
	(Protests against these statements are expected and welcome. Bitte auf deutsch!)

A NOW IT'S YOUR TURN. DEVELOP YOUR OWN LOW-RISK CHARACTERS by using the sentences above as cues. You may vary the verb, the rest of the sentence, or add completely new statements.

B MORE CHANCES TO UNLOAD CLICHÉS AND STEREOTYPES.

Frauen
Männer
Kinder
Katzen
Politiker

Wer kocht hier? Wer lernt hier? Warum lernen die Männer kochen? Was sagt die Frau? (speculate) Was sagen die Männer? (speculate)

ESSENTIAL GRAMMAR: Present Tense of *haben, sein, machen.*

haben	sein	machen
ich habe	ich bin	ich mache
du hast	du bist	du machst
er	er	er
sie hat	sie ist	sie macht
es	es	es
wir haben	wir sind	wir machen
ihr habt	ihr seid	ihr macht
Sie haben	Sie sind	Sie machen
sie haben	sie sind	sie machen

Kapitel 3

HUCKEBEIN —

DER UNGLÜCKSRABE

If you are a curious person, you will probably be a very good language learner. Your curiousity about other people and the world around you will make each new lesson a special challenge: "How do they say that in German anyway?" "I don't know how to say what I think, but let's see—I can at least ask a question about it." Your need to know, to make yourself understood will push you into the kind of linguistic exploration which is at the heart of language learning.

Pictures, especially picture sequences such as cartoons, encourage linguistic exploration. Using a sort of sign language, they serve as very tolerant conversation partners. They leave the labeling of persons, objects and activities to us, while, at the same time, they pique our curiosity and invite us to make conjectures about relationships that may or may not exist.

The following pictures are taken from the picture story "Hans Huckebein der Unglücksrabe" by Wilhem Busch, who is generally considered the German 19th-century ancestor of modern cartoonists.

HUCKEBEIN, DER UNGLÜCKSRABE

A **DESCRIBE WHAT YOU SEE** in these pictures by answering the questions.

s Unglück	misfortune, bad luck
r Rabe, -n	raven
r Ast, -̈e	limb, branch
r Baum, -̈e	tree
r Junge, -n	boy
e Mütze, -n	cap
r Korb, -̈e	basket

Wo sitzt der Rabe? _____

Wo steht der Junge? _____

Was trägt der Junge? _____

Wie ist der Rabe? _____

klettern	to climb
traurig	sad
gefährlich	dangerous
denken	to think
More words:	

_____

_____

Was macht der Junge?

Wo steht der Korb?

Ist der Junge traurig?

Was macht der Rabe?

Was denkt der Rabe?

Warum ist Klettern gefährlich?

Was denkt der Junge?

B SPECULATE WHAT WOULD OR COULD HAPPEN, for instance: the boy might get tired, weak, angry, bored etc.; a neighbor, friend, relative, stranger, dog etc. might arrive; the boy might fall, cry, have to go to the toilet etc.; the raven might leave, attack, start talking, call his friends etc. BE IMAGINATIVE. You may humanize the animal.

EXAMPLE: Vielleicht wird der Junge müde.

Vielleicht

C DESCRIBE WHAT IS HAPPENING in the following four pictures.

fallen   to fall
brechen   to break
r Kopf, ⸚e   head

e Beere, -n   berry

Wohin fällt der Junge?
Was macht der Rabe?
Andere Kommentare:

zwischen   between
e Hose   pants

reacts

Wie reagiert° der Junge?
Kommentare über den
Raben, bitte!
Wo steht der Junge?

froh   happy
stecken   to put into, to be
   stuck in

Der Rabe hat keinen Kopf
mehr. Wo steckt der Kopf?
Warum ist der Junge froh?
Was denkt der Rabe?
Wie ist das Wetter?
Scheint die Sonne?

D We are skipping a few pictures and will tell you **HOW THE STORY GOES ON.**

Fritz (so heißt der Junge) bringt den Raben zu Tante Lotte.
Bei Tante Lotte macht der Rabe viel Unsinn.°   *"makes nonsense",*
                                                        messes up
Der Rabe beißt Tante Lotte in den Finger.
Der Rabe stiehlt° einem Hund den Knochen.   *steals*
Der Rabe kämpft° mit dem Hund um den Knochen.   *fights*
Huckebein beißt den Hund in den Schwanz.°   *tail*
Huckebein läuft über die Wäsche° und macht sie schmutzig.   *wash, laundry*
Er spielt mit den Tellern.
Die Teller fallen auf den Boden und zerbrechen.°   *break*
Er spielt mit Eiern.
Die Eier fallen auf den Boden und zerbrechen.
Er gießt° der Tante Bier in die Schuhe.
Die Tante wird böse.°   *pours*
Nun kommt das Ende: *angry*

Der Rabe sieht ein Glas voll Likör.
Was denkt der Rabe?

"_____?"

"Schmeckt_____?"

"_____?"

"Das riecht_____."

Der Rabe steckt° seinen Schnabel _____.   *puts, places*

samples, tries	Er probiert° _____?
reacts	Wie reagiert° Ihrer Meinung nach der Rabe?
	Er sagt: „_____.''
	Er trinkt _____.
	Er macht seine Augen zu.
	Es schmeckt so gut.
	_____
	Der Rabe hebt das Glas.
	Er trinkt es aus.
	Antialkoholiker sagen:
	Freunde des Alkohols sagen:
	_____!
	_____!
wings	Der Rabe hebt die Flügel.°
	Er versucht _____.
	Wo liegt das Glas? _____
	Was denkt der Rabe?
	_____
	Der Rabe steht auf _____.
drunk	Der Rabe ist betrunken.°
	Was macht er? _____
	Was denken Sie in diesem Moment?
	_____

Der Rabe ist betrunken.

Er fällt auf _____.

Wie geht es ihm? _____

Wer kann ihm helfen? _____

Der Rabe ist kein Schneider, aber er spielt mit Nadel und Faden.°   *thread*

Er wickelt° den Faden um _____.   *wraps ... around*
Was passiert vielleicht?

Vielleicht _____.

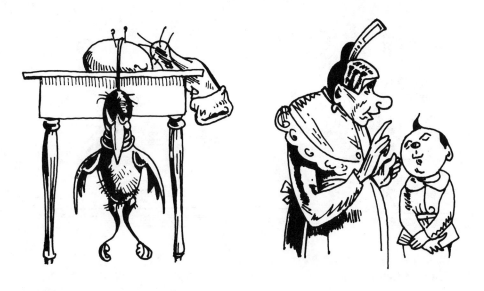

Der Rabe ist _____.
Sind Sie traurig? Ja? Warum?
                Nein? Warum nicht?

_____

_____

_____

Was sagt die Tante zu dem Jungen?

"Alkohol _____"

"_____"

"Der Rabe _____"

E RETELL THE PICTURE STORY, as a group effort or all by yourself. Cover the printed part of the page.

F STATE YOUR OPINION.

Sind sie für den Raben?

Sie Sie gegen Tante Lotte?

guilty   Ist Fritz schuldig?°

punishment   Ist die Strafe° für den Raben gerecht?°
just (appropriate)

                Ist die Strafe zu hart? Viele Fragen.

MAX UND MORITZ: Langeweile° und Protest

boredom

Es gibt noch andere Bildergeschichten mit Text von Wilhelm Busch. Eine Geschichte ist in Deutschland besonders populär. Sie heißt Max und Moritz. Max und Moritz sind eigentlich wie alle Jungen. Sie finden die Schule ziemlich langweilig. Sie finden das Leben auf dem Dorf ziemlich langweilig. Da ist nichts los:° kein Fußball, kein Fernsehen, keine Diskothek, keine Videospiele. Auch Motorräder gibt es noch nicht.

Nothing is going on there.

Die Erwachsenen° arbeiten und haben nicht viel Zeit für die Kinder. Frau Bolte hat Hühner. Sie lebt für ihre Hühner. Der Schneider, Herr Böck, näht Hosen, Mäntel und Anzüge. Der Lehrer, Herr Hempel, unterrichtet Deutsch, Mathematik und andere Fächer. Am Sonntag spielt er in der Kirche° Orgel.° Es gibt auch einen Onkel Fritz. Von seinem Beruf wissen wir nichts. Vielleicht ist er schon pensioniert.° Wahrscheinlich liest er jeden Tag die Zeitung, raucht seine Pfeife und ißt gut. Er schläft sehr gern in einem Federbett mit einer Mütze auf dem Kopf. Der Bäcker im Dorf ist dick. Kein Wunder! Denn sein Brot, seine Brötchen° und sein Kuchen schmecken ausgezeichnet. Auch der Müller° ist dick. Kein Wunder!° Seine Mühle° arbeitet für ihn.

the adults

church
organ
retired

roll
miller
No wonder!
mill

Max und Moritz sind mit ihrem Leben auf dem Dorf nicht zufrieden. Sie spielen den Erwachsenen Streiche,° d.h. sie ärgern° die Erwachsenen. Heute sagen wir: sie rebellieren gegen die Welt der Erwachsenen, gegen die Gesellschaft,° gegen das System.

play tricks
annoy
society

WITWE° BOLTE

widow

Zunächst° sterben die Hühner von Frau Bolte—ein Sabotageakt von Max und Moritz. Dann brät Frau Bolte die Hühner. Aber Max und Moritz stehlen° sie. Die Methode ist ziemlich interessant. (Siehe nächste Seite)

first
steal

A ANALYSE: WAS ZEIGT DAS BILD?

Wen sehen Sie auf dem Bild? _____

Wo sind Max und Moritz? _____

Wem gehören die Hühner? _____

Wo ist Frau Bolte? _____

Wo ist der Hund? _____

Was macht Frau Bolte? _____

Was macht der Hund? _____

USEFUL WORDS

s Dach	roof
r Keller	basement
e Küche	kitchen
angeln	to fish
fischen	
s Sauer-	sauerkraut
kraut	
holen	to fetch
bellen	to bark
springen	to jump

frying pan

B SPEKULATION: WAS PASSIERT VIELLEICHT? Frau Bolte geht in die Küche.
Nur noch drei Hühner sind in der Bratpfanne.°

Was denkt sie?

Was sagt sie?

Was tut sie?

SCHNEIDER BÖCK

Max und Moritz ärgern° Herrn Böck, den Schneider. Sie rufen ihn bei seinem Spitznamen:° "Ziegen-Böck"°. Der Schneider wird böse.° Er kommt mit einem Stock aus dem Haus und läuft über die Brücke. Auf dem Bild sehen Sie das Resultat.°

annoy
by his nickname
take-off on
Ziegenbock - billy
goat
angry
result

A **JETZT FRAGEN *SIE:*** Geben Sie auch eine Antwort.

Ask why the bridge breaks.

_____ ? _____

Ask what is happening to Mr. Böck.

_____ ?

Ask what Max and Moritz are doing.

_____ ? _____

Ask what Mr. Böck is thinking.

_____ ? _____

Ask how the water is.

_____ ? _____

B Das Wasser ist kalt. **WAS IST DAS RESULTAT?**

Herr Böck

USEFUL WORDS

frieren	to freeze
eine	to catch
Erkältung	cold
bekommen	
ertrinken	to drown
hassen	to hate

C **FORM AN ASSOCIATIVE CHAIN:**

Wasser –

D Wasser ist wichtig. **ERKLÄREN SIE WARUM.**

EXAMPLE: Wir brauchen Wasser   zum Trinken.
                                                        zum Kochen.

LEHRER HEMPEL

Herr Hempel, der Lehrer, raucht gern Pfeife. Max und Moritz stopfen die Pfeife mit Schießpulver.° Herr Hempel kommt aus der Kirche. (Sie wissen: dort spielt er am Sonntag Orgel.) Er ist mit seiner Arbeit zufrieden und denkt: „Und jetzt eine schöne Pfeife!" Er nimmt ein Streichholz und . . . Auf dem Bild sehen Sie das Resultat. Zum Glück passiert nicht viel. Er bekommt einen Schreck° und sein Gesicht wird schwarz. Das ist alles.

gunpowder

to get a shock (scare)

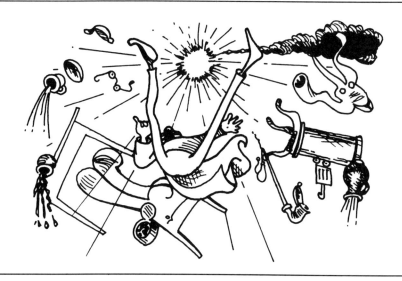

A WAS IST HIER LOS?

Die Pfeife

Der Kaffee

Der Ofen

Der Lehrer

Der Sessel

Die Tasse

Die Kaffeekanne

USEFUL WORDS

fliegen	to fly
explodieren	to explode
fließen	to flow
durch die Luft	through the air
gegen die Wand	against the wall
r Boden	the floor

B The picture illustrates an unusual situation. **TELL US WHERE THE PERSON AND THE OBJECTS CAN BE FOUND UNDER NORMAL CIRCUMSTANCES.**

usually

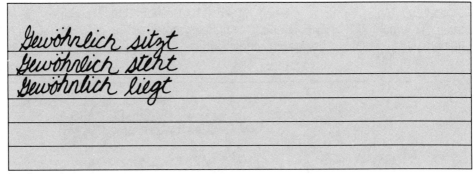

Gewöhnlich sitzt
Gewöhnlich steht
Gewöhnlich liegt

INSTANT SUCCESS IN VOCABULARY BUILDING

explodieren   to explode
Many German verbs are of Latin or Greek origin. They end in **-ieren** and usually mean the same as their English equivalents.

A WRITE THE GERMAN VERBS IN THE SPACE PROVIDED.

to protest	**protestieren**
to export	**exportieren**
to import	_____
to inform	_____
to add	_____ (math only)
to telephone	**telephonieren**
to divide	_____ (math only)
to improvise	_____
to repair	**reparieren**
to eliminate	**eliminieren**
to delegate	_____
to marinate	_____
to ventilate	_____
to navigate	_____
to compensate	_____
to multiply	**multiplizieren**

to ratify	**ratifizieren**
to identify	_____
to verify	_____
to qualify	_____
to copy	**kopieren**
to study	_____
to photograph	**photographieren**
to telegraph	**telegraphieren**
to discuss	**diskutieren**
to program	**programmieren**
to abstract	**abstrahieren**
to march	**marschieren**
to criticize	**kritisieren**

B ASK YOUR CLASSMATES QUESTIONS with the words above and expect answers.

ONKEL FRITZ

Diese Episode ist bei Kindern (und Erwachsenen) in Deutschland besonders beliebt°. *popular*
Denn alle kennen und lieben Maikäfer.° Kinder sammeln sie, nehmen sie mit in die *May beetle*
Schule und lassen sie in der Klasse fliegen. Das ärgert die Lehrer und macht den
Kindern Spaß. Die Maikäfer landen auf den Tischen, den Gardinen° und manchmal *curtain*
auf dem Kopf des Lehrers. Das ist natürlich der Höhepunkt° der Stunde. Max und *climax*
Moritz stecken ein paar Käfer° bei Onkel Fritz ins Bett. Auf dem Bild sehen Sie das *beetle*
Resultat.

A FRAGEN ZUM BILD: ONKEL FRITZ, MAIKÄFER UND FEDERBETTEN

Wo liegt Onkel Fritz? _____

Schläft er gut? Ja? Warum? Nein? Warum nicht?_____

Wie finden Sie Federbetten?_____

Warum schläft Onkel Fritz mit einer Mütze auf dem Kopf?_____

Wieviele Maikäfer sehen Sie?_____

Wo ist Maikäfer Nr. 1?_____

B Sie sind Onkel Fritz. **WAS MACHEN SIE JETZT?** After one of your classmates has proposed a course of action for Uncle Fritz, try to **SHOW THE FUTILITY OF THIS ACTION** by an appropriate statement. Several statements are invited.

EXAMPLE: schreien

Ich schreie laut.

Maikäfer hören schlecht.
Kein Mensch ist im Haus.

Proposed action

Why it does not work

USEFUL WORDS
um Hilfe rufen
aus dem Bett
springen
Licht machen
den Käfer fangen
mit dem Käfer
sprechen
Insektenspray holen
mit der Polizei
telephonieren
unter das Bett
kriechen
beten
den Käfer töten
aus dem
Schlafzimmer laufen
ein Glas Wein
trinken

C **ASK YOUR CLASSMATES** about their personal taste. They should support their judgment with an explanation.

> EXAMPLE: Wie findest du Maikäfer? Ich finde Maikäfer interessant. Man kann mit ihnen spielen.
> Wie findest du . . .

Herrn Reagan?   Dolly Parton   Rauschgift   Alkohol   Shakespeare   Deutschland

Hockey   Billy Martin   die Universität   Krieg   Comics   "Dallas"   Lederhosen°   *leather shorts or pants*

McDonalds   Sozialismus   Kommunismus

interessant   häßlich°   niedlich°   teuer   süß   aggressiv   intelligent   idiotisch   *ugly*
cute

schön   gefährlich   provozierend   dumm   verführerisch°   unmoralisch°   nötig   *seductive*
immoral

aktiv   langweilig   vulgär   arrogant   mutig°   *courageous*

D Und Episode Nummer° 5 und Nummer 6? Vielleicht erzählt Ihnen Ihr Professor   *number*
Episode Nummer 5 und 6. Oder noch besser: vielleicht **LESEN SIE EINMAL MAX UND MORITZ IM ORIGINAL.** Die Bilder machen es leicht.

E Look at the picture on p. 31. **SPECULATE ABOUT MR. BÖCK COMING HOME.** What could his wife say?

_____

What is going on?
_____

Why are you so wet?
_____

Are you sick?
_____

Are you crazy?
_____

It is too cold for swimming.
_____

You are not a fish.

F **RETELL THE FOUR TRICKS** that Max and Moritz play on Frau Bolte, Herrn Böck, Herrn Hempel und Onkel Fritz.

Ready for another joke with and about two "Ostfriesen"? If you need an introduction to this kind of humor, turn to KAPITEL 1, p. 5.
Der Ostfriese Hajo fragt den Ostfriesen Enno:
"Glaubst du, auf dem Mond wohnen Leute?"
Enno antwortet:° "Natürlich, da oben brennt doch Licht!"

answers

ESSENTIAL GRAMMAR: Verbs with Stem Vowel Change; *wo* or *wohin*

Some of the most frequently used German verbs change the stem vowel e and a in the second and third person singular:
a changes to **ä**
e changes to **i** or **ie**

schlafen	**essen**	**sehen**
ich schlafe	ich esse	ich sehe
du schläfst	du ißt	du siehst
er	er	er
sie schläft	sie ißt	sie sieht
es	es	es
wir schlafen	wir essen	wir sehen
ihr schlaft	ihr eßt	ihr seht
Sie schlafen	Sie essen	Sie sehen
sie schlafen	sie essen	sie sehen

 A Below is a list of other frequently used verbs that behave in the same way **FILL IN THE BASIC ENGLISH MEANING OF THESE VERBS.**

fahren＿＿＿＿	brechen＿＿＿＿	befehlen＿＿＿＿
fallen＿＿＿＿	geben＿＿＿＿	geschehen＿＿＿＿
fangen＿＿＿＿	helfen＿＿＿＿	lesen＿＿＿＿
halten＿＿＿＿	nehmen＿＿＿＿	stehlen＿＿＿＿
lassen＿＿＿＿	sprechen＿＿＿＿	
schlagen＿＿＿＿	sterben＿＿＿＿	
tragen＿＿＿＿	werden＿＿＿＿	
verlassen＿＿＿＿	werfen＿＿＿＿	
wachsen＿＿＿＿	treffen＿＿＿＿	
waschen＿＿＿＿	vergessen＿＿＿＿	

B WRITE SENTENCES that contrast the vowel change.

EXAMPLE: Ich fahre nach Italien. Wohin fährst du?
Ich trage einen Pullover. Was trägt er (sie)?

Wo or wohin? dative or accusative?

1. **Wo steht der Junge?**   **Unter dem Baum**. (dative)
(Where is the boy standing?)   (under the tree)

2. **Wohin fällt der Junge?**   **In den Korb**. (accusative)
(Where is the boy falling?)   (into the basket)

Standing under a tree (1) is a stationary activity. The boy remains in one place (under the tree), he is not moving toward a different location. Question: **Wo?** Answer in the dative.

Falling from a tree (2) definitely involves motion from one location to another: the boy is falling from the branch into the basket. Question: **Wohin?** Answer in the accusative. The decision between **wo?** (remaining in one place, dative) and **wohin?** (moving from one location to another, accusative) has to be made when using the following nine "two-way" prepositions:

an	at the side of, by, at, on
auf	on top of, on
hinter	behind
in	in, inside of, into
neben	next to, beside, by
über	over, above, about, across
unter	under, among
vor	in front of, before
zwischen	between

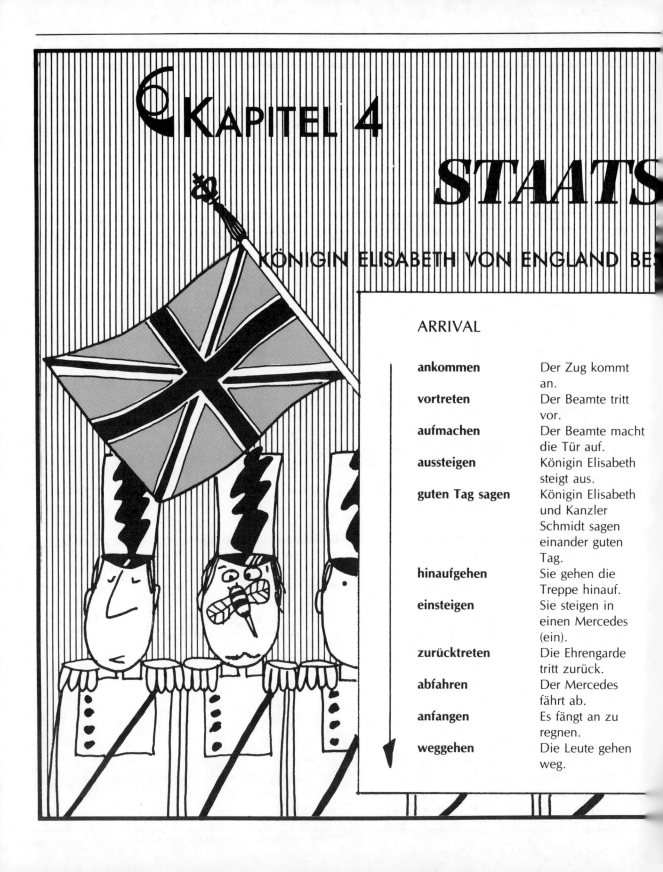

KAPITEL 4

STAATS

ARRIVAL

ankommen	Der Zug kommt an.
vortreten	Der Beamte tritt vor.
aufmachen	Der Beamte macht die Tür auf.
aussteigen	Königin Elisabeth steigt aus.
guten Tag sagen	Königin Elisabeth und Kanzler Schmidt sagen einander guten Tag.
hinaufgehen	Sie gehen die Treppe hinauf.
einsteigen	Sie steigen in einen Mercedes (ein).
zurücktreten	Die Ehrengarde tritt zurück.
abfahren	Der Mercedes fährt ab.
anfangen	Es fängt an zu regnen.
weggehen	Die Leute gehen weg.

BESUCH

...CHT KANZLER HELMUT SCHMIDT IN BONN.

DEPARTURE

Der Zug fährt ab.	**abfahren**
Der Beamte tritt zurück.	**zurücktreten**
Der Beamte macht die Tür zu.	**zumachen**
Die Königin steigt ein.	**einsteigen**
Königin Elisabeth und Kanzler Schmidt sagen einander auf Wiedersehen.	**auf Wiedersehen sagen**
Sie gehen die Treppe hinunter.	**hinuntergehen**
Sie steigen aus dem Mercedes (aus).	**aussteigen**
Die Ehrengarde tritt vor.	**vortreten**
Der Mercedes kommt an.	**ankommen**
Es hört auf zu regnen.	**aufhören**
Die Leute kommen zurück.	**zurückkommen**

A RETRACE THE EVENTS, first the arrival, then the departure. Don't look at the sentences but cue one another by reading out the infinitives in sequence. If separable verbs pose a problem, turn to the grammar survey at the end of this chapter.

B A group of students may **PANTOMIME THE EVENTS** and have the class provide the corresponding statement in German.

C DESCRIBE SOME OF THE EVENTS MORE SPECIFICALLY by adding more information. Limit yourself to one item:

finally
delay
track

1. Der Zug kommt ＿＿＿＿＿＿＿＿＿＿＿ an.
   (endlich,° langsam, mit Verspätung,° um 10 Uhr 20, auf dem Bahnhof, in Bonn, auf Gleis 2° ...)

2. Der Beamte tritt ＿＿＿＿＿＿＿＿＿＿＿ vor.
   (langsam, schnell, müde, ohne Mütze ...)

cautious
smiling

3. Königin Elisabeth steigt ＿＿＿＿＿＿＿＿＿＿＿ aus.
   (vorsichtig,° lächelnd,° nach zwei Minuten, ohne Prinz Philip, mit einem Pudel ...)

conversation
umbrella

4. Sie gehen ＿＿＿＿＿＿＿＿＿＿＿ die Treppe hinauf.
   (zusammen, im Gespräch,° mit den Diplomaten, ohne Regenschirm° ...)

a few

5. Es fängt ＿＿＿＿＿＿＿＿＿＿＿ an zu regnen.
   (plötzlich, nach ein paar° Minuten, jetzt, wieder, langsam, leider ...)

disappointed
groups

6. Die Leute gehen ＿＿＿＿＿＿＿＿＿＿＿ weg.
   (langsam, zufrieden, enttäuscht,° in Gruppen,° bei Regen, mit Regenschirmen, mit Freunden ...)

7. Die Leute kommen ＿＿＿＿＿＿＿＿＿＿＿ zurück.
   (neugierig, mit Regenmänteln, mit Freunden ...)

D FORM ASSOCIATIVE CHAINS with: 1) Königin Elisabeth, 2) Mercedes, 3) Es fängt an zu regnen.

E RESPOND TO THE PHOTO of Queen Elizabeth.

angry

Warum ist die Königin böse?° ＿＿＿＿＿＿＿＿＿＿＿＿＿＿＿＿＿＿＿＿＿
Was denkt sie von Herrn Schmidt?

Sie denkt: "_____."

Was denkt sie von Frau Thatcher?

Sie denkt: "_____."

Wo ist die Königin? _____

Ist sie bei einem Staatsbesuch?

Warum? _____.

Warum nicht? _____.

Sieht sie wie eine Königin aus?

Warum? _____.

Warum nicht? _____.

Warum trägt sie ein Kopftuch?° _____.   *kerchief, head-scarf*

Warum ist Helmut Schmidt nicht bei ihr? _____.

Wo sind die Zuschauer?° _____.   *spectators*

Warum sehen wir keine Limousine? _____.

Warum ist Prinz Philip nicht da? _____ .

Wo ist die Musik? _____ .

Wen sieht die Königin? _____ .

Was sieht sie? _____ .

Wie alt ist die Königin? _____ .

Wie ist das Wetter? _____ .

F Herr Schmidt und Frau Thatcher haben Geheimnisse. Was sagen Herr Schmidt und Frau Thatcher zueinander? **ERFINDEN SIE MÖGLICHE ANTWORTEN.**

HERR SCHMIDT: Wann machen Sie Ferien, Frau Thatcher?

FRAU THATCHER: _____

FRAU THATCHER: Gehen Sie heute abend ins Theater?

HERR SCHMIDT: _____

governs HERR SCHMIDT: Wer regiert° England, Sie oder die Königin?

FRAU THATCHER: _____

FRAU THATCHER: Morgen bleibe ich zu Haus. Die Konferenz ist sehr langweilig.

HERR SCHMIDT: _____

HERR SCHMIDT: Wieviel verdienen Sie pro Jahr?

FRAU THATCHER: _____

FRAU THATCHER: Warum gibt es in Deutschland keinen Plumpudding?

HERR SCHMIDT: _____

HERR SCHMIDT: Wann hört Herr Reagan endlich auf? Er spricht schon eine Stunde.

FRAU THATCHER: _____

FRAU THATCHER: Was halten° Sie von Königin Elisabeth?   *think of*

HERR SCHMIDT: _____

HERR SCHMIDT: In zwei Minuten rufe ich meinen Chauffeur.

FRAU THATCHER: _____

FRAU THATCHER: Ich fliege morgen nach London zurück. Kommen Sie mit?

HERR SCHMIDT: _____

HELMUT SCHMIDT BESUCHT RONALD REAGAN:
Staatsbesuch im Weißen Haus

Die Sonne scheint. Der Himmel ist blau. Das Musikkorps° spielt. Ronald Reagan,   *band*
Präsident der Vereinigten Staaten,° wartet. Neben ihm wartet Nancy Reagan, seine   *the United States*
Frau. Sie hat ein sehr elegantes Kleid an. Sie lächelt.° Sie ist 60. Aber sie sieht noch   *smiles*
sehr jung aus. Ronald Reagan ist 72 Jahre alt. Er sieht etwas müde aus. Der Teppich
ist rot. Er ist für Helmut Schmidt. Eine Limousine kommt vor dem Weißen Haus an.
Sie ist schwarz. Die Musik hört jetzt auf. Die Türen der Limousine gehen auf.°   *open*
Helmut Schmidt steigt aus. Er hat eine blaue Mütze auf.° Er ist freundlich. Er lächelt.   *has on*
Er winkt den Zuschauern zu.° Ein Polizist macht die Türen der Limousine zu. Die   *waves to*
Limousine fährt ab. Helmut Schmidt geht Ronald Reagan entgegen.° Ronald Reagan   *walks toward*
geht Helmut Schmidt entgegen. Helmut Schmidt nimmt seine Mütze ab. Präsident
Reagan stellt dem Bundeskanzler seine Frau vor. Nancy Reagan sagt: „Wie geht es
Ihnen, Herr Bundeskanzler?" Helmut Schmidt antwortet: „Danke, gut. Und Ihnen,
Frau Reagan?"

Dann hält Ronald Reagan eine Rede.° Er spricht von der Freundschaft° zwischen   *gives a speech*
Deutschland und Amerika. Er lobt das deutsche Bier und die deutschen Autos.   *friendship*
Helmut Schmidt hört gut zu. Die Rede ist jetzt zu Ende. Die Zuschauer° klatschen.   *spectators*
Jetzt hält Helmut Schmidt eine Rede. Er spricht von der Freundschaft zwischen
Amerika und Deutschland. Er lobt das amerikanische Steak und die amerikanischen
Raketen.° Die Rede ist zu Ende. Wieder klatschen° die Zuschauer. Ronald Reagan   *rockets/applaud*

shake hands

watch, pay attention
watch
joke

und Helmut Schmidt schütteln einander die Hände.° Die Pressephotographen photographieren. Die Reporter schreiben sehr schnell. Die Polizisten passen sehr gut auf.° Die Zuschauer schauen zu.° Ronald Reagan erzählt einen Witz,° und Helmut Schmidt lacht.

Ein Beamter macht die Tür zum Weißen Haus auf. Nancy, Ronald und Helmut gehen hinein.

Die Musik fängt wieder an. Die Zuschauer gehen weg. Im Weißen Haus gehen die Lichter an.

A RETRACE THE EVENTS at the White House with the cues provided. You do not have to reproduce the text literally. Always pronounce the complete statement. You may want to leave the blanks empty for repeated oral practice in class.

Die Sonne _____. Der Himmel _____. _____ spielt. Ronald

Reagan _____. Neben ihm _____. _____ ein

sehr elegantes Kleid _____. Sie _____. _____ 60.

_____ noch sehr jung aus. _____ 74 _____ alt. Er

_____ etwas müde _____. _____ rot. Er ist für _____.

_____ kommt vor dem Weißen Haus _____. _____ schwarz.

Die Musik _____. Die Türen _____ gehen _____. Helmut

Schmidt steigt _____. Er _____ eine blaue Mütze _____.

_____ freundlich. _____ lächelt. Er winkt _____ zu. Ein

Polizist macht _____. Die Limousine _____ ab. Helmut Schmidt

_____ Ronald Reagan _____. Ronald Reagan _____ Helmut

Schmidt _____. Helmut Schmidt _____ seine Mütze _____.

Präsident Reagan _____ dem Bundeskanzler _____ vor. Nancy Rea-

gan sagt: "_____?" Helmut Schmidt antwortet:

"_____?"

Dann _____ Ronald Reagan eine Rede. Er _____ von der Freund-

schaft zwischen Deutschland und Amerika. Er lobt das _____ und die

_____. Helmut Schmidt _____ gut _____. Die Rede ist jetzt

_____. Die Zuschauer _____. Jetzt _____ Helmut Schmidt

_____. Er _____ von der Freundschaft _____ Deutschland

und Amerika. Er lobt das _____ und die _____. Die Rede ist

_____. Wieder _____ die Zuschauer. Ronald Reagan und Helmut

Schmidt schütteln einander _____. Die Pressephotographen _____.

Die Reporter _____ sehr schnell. Die Polizisten _____ sehr gut

_____. Die Zuschauer _____ zu. Ronald Reagan _____

einen Witz, und Helmut Schmidt _____.

Ein Beamter _____ die Tür zum Weißen Haus _____. Nancy, Ronald

und Helmut gehen _____.

Die Musik fängt wieder _____. Die Zuschauer _____ wieder

_____. Im Weißen Haus _____ die Lichter.

B PLAY WITH POSSIBILITIES

1. Die Sonne scheint. Was machen Sie?
   Ich spiele Tennis.

   Ich _____.

   Ich _____.

   Ich _____.

2.   Ronald Reagan ...

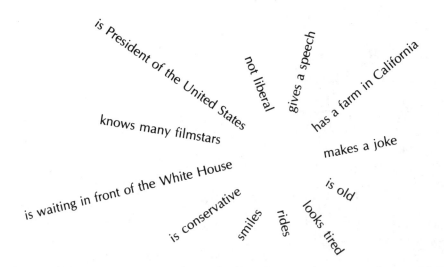

3.   Helmut Schmidt ...

4. Präsident Reagan und Kanzler Schmidt sitzen im Weißen Haus am Tisch.

   Sie sprechen über _____

   Sie lachen. Warum? _____

   Beide sehen _____ aus. Warum?

   _____

   Frau Reagan sagt: "Ronnie, du trinkst _____.

                  Du ißt _____.

                  Du sprichst _____."

                  "Du _____."

   Herr Schmidt sagt: "Frau Reagan, ich finde Sie _____

   Nancy Reagan steht plötzlich auf. Warum? _____

C RETELL HELMUT SCHMIDT'S ARRIVAL IN BAD WEATHER. You may use the English cues and/or your own ideas.

1. Die Sonne _____.
   (does not shine, is not there, is not visible, is behind clouds ...)

2. Der Himmel _____.
   (is grey, dark, black, without sun, overcast, not blue ...)

3. Das Musikkorps _____.
   (does not play, plays badly, is sitting in the White House, is sitting under a tree, in a bus, is not there, plays records ...)

4. Ronald Reagan _____.
   (is waiting under an umbrella, in the White House, in a car, is putting on his swimsuit, likes the rain, is mad ...)

5. Nancy Reagan _____.
   (does not smile, is angry, is holding an umbrella, opens an umbrella, flies to California, is drinking coffee ...)

6. Sie hat _____ an.
   (a raincoat, a winter coat, a bathrobe, a swimsuit ...)

7. Sie sieht _____ aus.
   (elegant, nervous, unhappy, good, sick, old ...)

8. Ronald Reagan sieht _____ aus.
   (young, old, tired, interesting, wet, curious ...)

9. Der Teppich ist _____.
   (wet, dirty, not there, too wet for Helmut Schmidt, dangerous ...)
   Es regnet, donnert° und blitzt.°

there is thunder
there is lightening

10. Eine Limousine _____.
    (comes through the rain, drives past the White House and does not stop, stops in the rain, drives over the carpet ...)

11. Das Musikkorps _____.
    (runs away, goes home, is standing under a tree, goes into the White House, buys umbrellas, needs a boat ...)

12. Helmut Schmidt _____.
    (does not get out, is waiting in the car, stays in the limousine, smokes a cigarette, likes rain, calls Reagan on the phone, drinks a glass of wine, listens to music, puts on a swimsuit ...)

D You are a reporter interviewing Helmut Schmidt. **ASK SOME QUESTIONS.**
One half of the class may be the "collective mind" of the reporter, the other
half the "collective mind" of Helmut Schmidt. There may be several answers to one
question. Use the English cues and make up your own questions, in German, of
course!

REPORTER: How are you?

HELMUT SCHMIDT: _____.
REPORTER: Do you speak English?

HELMUT SCHMIDT: _____.
REPORTER: Are you tired?

HELMUT SCHMIDT: _____.
REPORTER: How long will you stay? (present tense)

HELMUT SCHMIDT: _____.
REPORTER: How do you like America?

HELMUT SCHMIDT: _____.
REPORTER: Who pays for the visit?

HELMUT SCHMIDT: _____.
REPORTER: Why do you wear a cap?

HELMUT SCHMIDT: _____
REPORTER: Why are you coming to America?

HELMUT SCHMIDT: _____
REPORTER: Do you bring money?

HELMUT SCHMIDT: _____
REPORTER: Do you play tennis?

HELMUT SCHMIDT: _____
REPORTER: When do you get up?

HELMUT SCHMIDT: _____
REPORTER: Do you love cats or dogs?

HELMUT SCHMIDT: _____
REPORTER: Do you have friends in Washington?

HELMUT SCHMIDT: _____
REPORTER: Do you need rockets?

HELMUT SCHMIDT: _____

REPORTER: _____

HELMUT SCHMIDT: _____

REPORTER: _____

HELMUT SCHMIDT: _____

E FIND AS MANY ANSWERS AS CAN BE PRODUCED COMFORTABLY.
Answers can be negated and contested. If the ensuing exchange breaks down return to simple unrelated statements or go on to the next question.

Warum hat Helmut Schmidt keine Mütze auf? _____

Warum winkt° Ronald Reagan? _____

Wem winkt Ronald Reagan zu? _____

Direkt hinter Ronald Reagan sehen Sie ein weißes Gebäude. Ist das das Weiße

Haus? Wenn nein, was ist das? _____ *waves*

Wie sieht Ronald Reagan aus? _____

Wo sind wir? _____

Wo sind die Zuschauer?° _____ *spectators*

Was liegt hinter den drei Männern? _____

Was machen die Leute auf dem Wachturm?° _____ *watchtower*

Nancy Reagan ist nicht da. Wo ist sie? *(Speculate wildly)* _____

Warum ist Ronald Reagan in Berlin? _____

Warum steht Helmut Schmidt neben Ronald Reagan? _____

Warum lächelt Herr Reagan? _____

Warum lächelt der Bürgermeister von Berlin, Herr Weizsäcker, nicht? _____

Warum steht auf dem Schild° „Achtung"?° _____ *sign attention*

F HERR SCHMIDT DIRIGIERT Try to establish the locale. Interpret the picture by attributing possible thoughts to the people involved. Direct simple questions to the people in the picture. Make use of the information provided by the texts and other pictures in this chapter. Mix private with public matters. Be imaginative!

Wo sind wir? _____

Warum lacht Jimmy Carter? _____

Was denkt Helmut Schmidt? _____

Was denken die Musiker? _____

Das Kleid von Frau Carter ... _____.

Fragen Sie Herrn Schmidt!

Was _____?

Wie _____?

Warum _____?

Was machen Carter und Schmidt nach dem Konzert? (Speculate wildly!)

_____

_____

Andere Fragen und Kommentare: _____

_____

_____

ESSENTIAL GRAMMAR: Separable Verbs

For speakers of English, the so-called separable verbs should not pose any problems, for the use of prepositions and adverbs to change the meaning of a verb is common to both languages. Compare:

He didn't *turn* once.

This music *turns* me *on*.

Wo *steht* das Auto?

Ich *stehe* um sieben *auf*.

In each instance the basic meaning of the verb has been changed through a preposition. The difference is that in German the preposition is attached to the infinitive as a prefix; in English the preposition stays separate.

The meaning of many separable German verbs can be derived from the primary meanings of the separable prefix and the verb to which it is attached. With growing experience in German you will be able to "guess" intelligently some less accessible meanings from the context.

Study the list of the most common prefixes with their primary meanings in given examples. It will prepare you to tackle separable German verbs with more confidence.

✳ **NOTE:** The accent is always on the prefix.

ab	off	**abfahren**	to drive off, leave
		abschalten	to switch off, turn off
an	at, on	**ansehen**	to look at
		ankommen	to arrive (at)
		anschalten	to switch on, turn on
auf	up, open	**aufstehen**	to get up
		aufessen	to eat up
		aufmachen	to open ("make open")
aus	out	**aussteigen**	to get out ("climb out")
ein	in, into	**einsteigen**	to get into ("climb in")
fort, weg	away	**fortgehen**	to go away
		wegnehmen	to take away
her	toward the speaker	**herkommen**	to come here

	("here" in the sense of "hither")		
hin	away from the speaker ("there" in the sense of "thither")	**hinfahren**	to drive there
mit	along, with	**mitnehmen**	to take along ("with")
nach	after (mainly in the sense of following, following up, checking up on an action)	**nachkommen**	to come after, to follow
		nachzählen	to count again (check the count)
		nachsehen	to check, look up
vor	before, ahead forward, in front of	**vorlegen**	to put before
		vorgehen	to go ahead, to go to the front
		vortreten	to step forward
zu	close (adding aspect of closing to various activities)	**zumachen**	to shut ("make closed")
	increase (adding aspect of increasing to various activities)	**zunehmen**	to "take on weight", to gain weight
zu	to	**zustimmen**	to agree to (adding your opinion to an existing one)
zurück	back	**zurückgeben**	to give back
zusammen	together	**zusammen-bleiben**	to stay together
		zusammen-kleben	to stick together, to paste together

Verbs acting like separable prefixes can be found in three frequently used expressions:

kennenlernen	to become acquainted with, meet
stehenbleiben	to stop, not move
spazierengehen	to go for a walk

Many verbal phrases behave like separable verbs, but their infinitive form is not written as one word. Like a separable prefix, the element preceding the infinitive goes to the very end of the sentence:

nach Hause gehen	to go home	Ich **gehe** heute um fünf **nach Hause**.
Tennis spielen	to play tennis	Heute **spiele** ich mit Erika **Tennis.**

In both examples, the preceding element makes the general activity "gehen" or "spielen" so much more explicit, that the new expression (**nach Hause gehen, Tennis spielen**) describes a clearly defined, different activity. It can be considered a new verb.

There are two main groups of verbal phrases that behave like separable verbs:

1. Verbs of motion (to come, to fly, to drive, to go, to travel, etc.) toward or from a place of activity:

nach Hause fahren	to drive home, go home
nach New York fliegen	to fly to New York
ins Kino gehen	to go to the movies
in die Kirche gehen	to go to church
ins Konzert gehen	to go to a concert
ins Theater gehen	to go to the theater
einkaufen gehen	to go shopping
essen gehen	to go and eat
schlafen gehen	to go to bed
zu Bett (ins Bett) gehen	to go to bed
aus Deutschland kommen	to come from Germany
nach Hause kommen	to come home
in Urlaub fahren	to go on vacation

2. Verbs describing a general activity (such as fahren, lernen, spielen, essen etc.) that are modified by another phrase to such an extent as to describe a distinct, specific activity.

Auto fahren	to drive a car
Motorrad fahren	to ride a motorcycle
Englisch lernen	to learn English
schwimmen lernen	to learn to swim
Mittag essen	to eat lunch
Fußball spielen	to play soccer
Tennis spielen	to play tennis
Gitarre spielen	to play the guitar
Klavier spielen	to play piano
Kaffee trinken	to have coffee

✳ NOTE:

radfahren	to ride a bike
skifahren	to ski

The infinitive shows them to be true separable verbs. But their origin from group 2 is still apparent in their finite form:

Ich **fahre** gern **Rad.**
Fahren Sie gern **Ski?**

A **MAKE UP YOUR MIND.** In class, read the problems to your fellow students who should answer with the books closed. Take turns.

1. Es ist zehn Uhr abends. Sie wollen lesen. Es ist dunkel. Schalten Sie das Licht an oder aus?

   Ich schalte das Licht _____.

2. Sie trinken jeden Tag sechs Liter Bier und essen drei Pizzas. Was passiert? Nehmen Sie zu oder ab?

   Ich nehme _____.

3. Es regnet. Sie wollen spazierengehen. Ziehen Sie Ihren Regenmantel an oder aus?

   Ich ziehe meinen Regenmantel _____.

to go on vacation 4. Sie fahren in Urlaub.° Schließen Sie die Haustür auf oder zu?

   Ich schließe die Haustür _____.

5. Sie hören Musik. Die Musik ist sehr langweilig. Schlafen Sie ein oder schlafen Sie aus?

   Ich schlafe _____.

6. Die Sowjets bauen mehr Raketen. Rüsten die Sowjets auf oder ab?

   Die Sowjets rüsten _____.

B **COMPLETE THE SENTENCE** with the appropriate prefix.

1. Königin Elisabeth verläßt Bonn. Der Zug hält. Die Königin steigt _____.

2. Heute abend gehen Sie mit Brigitte ins Kino. Was sagen Sie Ihren Eltern? Ich

   gehe mit Brigitte _____.

3. Morgen singt Michael Jackson in Chikago. Fahren Sie _____?

4. Was heißt "cucumber" auf deutsch? Sie wissen es nicht. Sie sehen im Wörter-

   buch _____.

5. Wir kennen Herrn Travolta noch nicht. Wir treffen ihn im Studio 54. Er spricht

   mit uns. Wir lernen Herrn Travolta _____.

6. Ein Professor schreibt schon fünf Stunden an einem Artikel. Der Professor

   braucht frische Luft. Was tut er? Er geht eine Stunde _____.

7. Viele Frauen lieben Robert Redford. Sie sagen: "Robert Redford sieht phantas-

   tisch _____."

8. In Aspen/Colorado laufen viele Amerikaner _____.

9. In Wimbledon spielt Herr McEnroe oft _____.

10. Bei der Tour de France fahren die Profis _____.

11. Ihre Eltern kennen Ihre Freundin Brigitte noch nicht. Was machen Sie? Ich

    stelle Brigitte meinen Eltern _____.

12. Nudisten lieben die Sonne, den Strand° und das Wasser. Nudisten haben nichts   *beach*

    _____.

13. Auf der Fifth Avenue in New York steht ein Elefant. Viele Leute bleiben

    neugierig° _____.   *curious*

14. Sie fahren an den Strand. Was nehmen Sie _____?

15. Sie machen Ferien in Deutschland. Es regnet schon seit drei Tagen. Sie sagen:

    "Wann hört der Regen endlich _____?"

KAPITEL 5

Tiere
Freunde
Verwandte

ICH BIN IMMER
ZUFRIEDEN – SOLANGE
ES MIR GUT GEHT.

JTM DAVIS

GARFIELD

Describing a funny pet, friend or relative can be a very challenging but rewarding task in the early stages of learning a foreign language. Since the topic is close to your heart, you will easily remember the story you want to tell, in the order you want to tell it. Before you begin to tell your story to your class, explain any difficult words— those words that everyone must understand to follow your story. Be sure to keep it simple. No one will enjoy your story if it's too difficult for them to understand.

KATER GARFIELD

TANTE BERTHA

tomcat	Ich habe einen Kater.°	Ich habe eine Tante.
	Er heißt Garfield.	Sie heißt Bertha.
	Garfield ist drei Jahre alt.	Tante Bertha ist sechzig Jahre alt.
angel	Garfield sieht wie ein Tiger aus, wie ein Mini-Tiger.	Tante Bertha sieht wie ein Engel° aus, wie ein Super-Engel.
	Er schläft am liebsten auf dem Schrank.	Sie schläft am liebsten auf dem Sofa.
eats	Er frißt° gern Fisch und Kartoffeln.	Sie ißt gern Kuchen und Schlagsahne.°
whipped cream	Garfield frißt auch die Reste vom Mittagessen.	Tante Bertha ißt auch Vitamine und Yoghurt.
praises	Meine Mutter lobt° ihn dann und sagt:	Meine Mutter lobt sie dann und sagt:
	„Garfield, du bist ein guter Kater."	„Bertha, so bleibst du jung und frisch."
	Garfield trinkt manchmal auch Bier.	Tante Bertha trinkt manchmal auch Likör.
	Wir lachen dann und sagen:	Wir lachen dann und sagen:
drunkard, boozer	„Garfield, du kleiner Säufer."°	„Tante Bertha, du kleine alte Säuferin."

A **PREPARE A SIMILAR SKETCH** for oral presentation in class. Replace Garfield with your pet and Bertha with your favorite or most interesting relative or friend. Change the text accordingly but retain the sentence patterns. Although an aunt ordinarily does not sleep on top of the cabinet, it may be interesting to have her sleep there. It may provoke good questions from the class after you have presented your sketch.

B **WARUM? WARUM? WARUM?**
QUESTION: Warum schläft dein Onkel unter dem Tisch?
ANSWER: Mein Onkel trinkt zuviel Wein.

(Suggested persons and animals: dein Freund, Ihre Freundin, eure Katze, sein Onkel, ihre Tante, unser Opa,° eure Oma,° Ihr Vater, deine Mutter, seine Schwester, euer Vetter,° unsere Kusine,° dein Hamster, Ihr Vogel, ihr Pferd ...)

too much
grandfather
grandmother
male cousin
female cousin

Warum bleibt	zu Hause?
Warum fährt	nach Alaska?

Warum nimmt	Medizin?
Warum geht	zu Fuß?
Warum haßt	Katzen?
Warum trägt	Lederhosen?°
Warum trinkt	Wein?
Warum spielt	Karten?
Warum springt	ins Wasser?
Warum klettert	auf einen Baum?
Warum lernt	Chinesisch?

leather shorts or pants

C **SOMEONE OR SOMETHING IS MISSING.** Where would be the most likely place to look for the person or object? Give a brief explanation why.

EXAMPLE: Ich suche meinen Bruder in den Rocky Mountains. Er läuft gern Ski.

Here is a group of persons and objects from which to choose. Of course, you can make up your own.

meinen Freund, unser Auto, euren Opa, deine Boa constrictor, ihren Mercedes, Ihren Pudel, unsere Katze, eure Pferde, deine Schwestern, seinen Hund, unsere Oma, meinen Arzt, deine Freundin, eure Kusine

Possible locations that may help you with your answers or encourage you to invent your own:

in Deutschland	hinter unserem Haus	
bei uns	auf dem Dach	
im Park	bei McDonalds	
unter meinem Bett	in den Rocky Mountains	
im Supermarkt	in den Alpen°	*Alps*
in der Kirche°	an der See	*church*
im Weißen Haus	in unserer Garage	
vor meinem Fenster	auf der Bank	
bei euch	auf der Autobahn	
in einer Kneipe°	in eurer Küche	*(cheap) bar, "joint"*
im Film	im Fernsehen	
in der Oper	im Badezimmer°	*bathroom*

D GIVE REASONS WHY YOU LIKE A PET, a friend or a relative:

EXAMPLE: Ich habe meinen Onkel gern. Er hat Humor.

E ASK ONE ANOTHER ABOUT YOUR PREFERENCES. Expect an explanation for the stated preference. Change between **du** and **Sie** as appropriate or practical for exercise purposes.

best of all
cosy

EXAMPLE: Wo arbeiten Sie am liebsten?° Ich arbeite am liebsten zu Hause.
Da ist es gemütlich.°

beach
stadium
instruction, class

1. Wo oder wann essen Sie am liebsten? Warum?
   (zu Hause, bei McDonalds, in einem Restaurant, am Strand,° im Wald, im Stadion,° auf einem Schiff, im Bett, im Kino, beim Fernsehen, im Flugzeug, nach
   dem Sport, bei der Arbeit, beim Camping, während des Unterrichts,° im Park …)

2. Was lesen Sie am liebsten? Warum?
   (die Zeitung, Comics, Kurzgeschichten, den *National Enquirer, Dear Abby,*
   Reklamen, die Speisekarte°, Liebesromane°, die Telephonrechnung,°…)

menu
love stories,
romances
telephone bill

3. Wo machen Sie am liebsten Ferien? Warum?

   _____

4. Wen besuchen Sie am liebsten? Warum?

   _____

5. Was hören Sie am liebsten? Warum?

   _____

6. _____ am liebsten. Warum? _____

7. _____ am liebsten. Warum? _____

8. _____ am liebsten. Warum? _____

F   AN INTERVIEW WITH GARFIELD.

REPORTER: Guten Tag, Garfield! Wie geht es dir?
GARFIELD: Danke gut. Und dir?
REPORTER: Danke, auch gut. Garfield, warum schläfst du am liebsten auf dem
           Schrank?
GARFIELD: Da ist es warm und gemütlich. Niemand stört° mich.   *disturbs*
REPORTER: Wann stehst du gewöhnlich auf?
GARFIELD: Manchmal um zehn. Manchmal um zwölf. Heute vielleicht gar
           nicht.
REPORTER: Warum?
GARFIELD: Es regnet. Außerdem bin ich müde. Bier macht müde.
REPORTER: Ach so! Was macht deine Freundin?
GARFIELD: Ich weiß nicht. Es regnet. Ich bin müde. Heute bleibe ich zu Haus.
REPORTER: Na, dann gute Nacht, Garfield!

Der Reporter
fragt—
Sie antworten:
Lieben Sie Tiere?
Warum tragen Sie
eine Pelzjacke?
Haben Sie einen
Hund oder eine
Katze? Was frißt
Ihr Hund (Ihre
Katze)?

G PREPARE A SIMILAR CONVERSATION or interview with your pet, in writing. Have a classmate read the lines of the interviewer/reporter; you answer from memory. Reverse the process and act as the reporter/interviewer. You produce your lines from memory and a classmate reads the answers. This will prepare you for an improvised interview (group to group or one on one). A picture of your favorite pet may help to inspire questions and answers.

VON TIEREN UND MENSCHEN

Wir lieben Tiere; nicht alle Tiere, aber viele.

Wir füttern sie gut, manchmal zu gut.

pet Wir streicheln° sie.

Wir geben ihnen Namen.

In Deutschland heißen Katzen meistens Muschi, kleine Hunde heißen oft Waldi, große Hunde heißen oft Harras.

Wir gehen mit Hunden spazieren, mit Katzen nicht so oft.

Manchmal werden auch Tiere krank.

veterinarian Dann gehen wir mit ihnen zum Arzt, zum Tierarzt.°

A WORK AND PLAY WITH THE TEXT.

love, pet, spoil, buy, sell, take to the doctor, take for a walk, feed, idealize, ...

Wir _____Tiere.

_____

_____

B Welche Tiere kennen Sie? **MAKE A LIST.** (Consult your teacher or dictionary about gender and plurals, if in doubt.)

C **MAKE A STATEMENT ABOUT EACH ANIMAL ON YOUR LIST** and expect your classmates to add their comments.

D **WO GEHEN SIE MIT IHREM HUND (IHRER KATZE USW.) SPAZIEREN?**

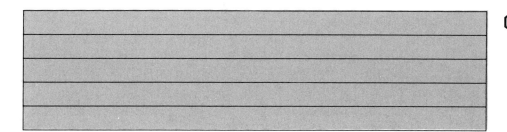
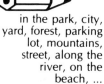

in the park, city, yard, forest, parking lot, mountains, street, along the river, on the beach, ...

Hunde helfen uns.
Sie bewachen° das Haus.
Sie holen ihrem Herrn die Zeitung.
Sie tragen ihrer Herrin die Einkaufstasche° nach Hause.
Hunde helfen der Polizei, Gangster und Heroin zu finden.
Bernhardiner retten Menschen aus tiefem Schnee.

watch, guard

shopping bag

A **WAS TUT IHR HUND** (Ihre Katze etc.)? Think of anything that is typical, unusual or noteworthy of your pet.

spoil

Manchmal verwöhnen° wir unsere Tiere.

Hunde und Katzen schlafen bei uns im Haus.

Oft liegen sie auf Stühlen, auf der Couch oder sogar im Bett.

Manche Damen stricken für ihren Hund einen Pullover oder kaufen ihm Steak.

Pudel gehen mit ihrem Herrn oder ihrer Herrin zum Hundesalon.

later
beauty contest

Später° besuchen sie einen Schönheitswettbewerb.°

Dort bekommen sie manchmal einen Preis.

A WIE VERWÖHNEN MANCHE ELTERN IHRE KINDER?

EXAMPLE: Sie kaufen ihnen alles.

1. _____

They give them a lot of spending money.

2. _____

They praise them all the time.

3. _____

They never criticize them.

4. _____

They ignore their flaws.

EXAMPLE: Sie lassen sie viel fernsehen.

1. Sie lassen sie _____.
   eat a lot of ice-cream

2. Sie lassen sie _____.
   always stay up late.

3. Sie lassen sie _____.
   always sleep late.

4. Sie lassen sie _____.
   go out twice a week.

5. Sie lassen sie _____.
   drink alcohol.

B Eine Dame strickt einen Pullover für ihren Hund. **WAS DENKT DER HUND?**

Mit einem Pullover sehe ich _____ aus.

good, elegant, interesting, stupid, crazy, rich,...

Der Pullover ist _____.

too warm, not practical, too long, too short, very tight, ridiculous, very beautiful,...

Ich hasse _____

Ich _____

Meine Herrin _____.

is sentimental, likes to work, loves me, has no taste, has too much time, spoils me, does not understand me, ...

C WO SCHLÄFT IHR HUND (Ihre Katze)?

under the bed

in the car

in the living room

behind the flowers

in the kitchen

on the refrigerator

near the door

in the bedroom

on the car

on the sofa

D BEIM FRISEUR warten viele Leute.

Beim Friseur _____.
          it is very warm.

Beim Friseur _____.
          it smells good.

Beim Friseur _____.
          I read newspapers and magazines.

Beim Friseur _____.
          I hear a lot of gossip.

Beim Friseur _____.

E WHERE DO YOU GO?

EXAMPLE: You want to eat. Wohin gehen Sie? Ich gehe ins Restaurant.

You want to dance, drink beer, take a train, take a plane, see a play, see a movie, see a soccer match, have coffee and cake, buy bread, buy fresh fish, go swimming, look at art, send a telegram, have your suit cleaned. You need money. You need a haircut. You are sick. You have no idea what to buy.

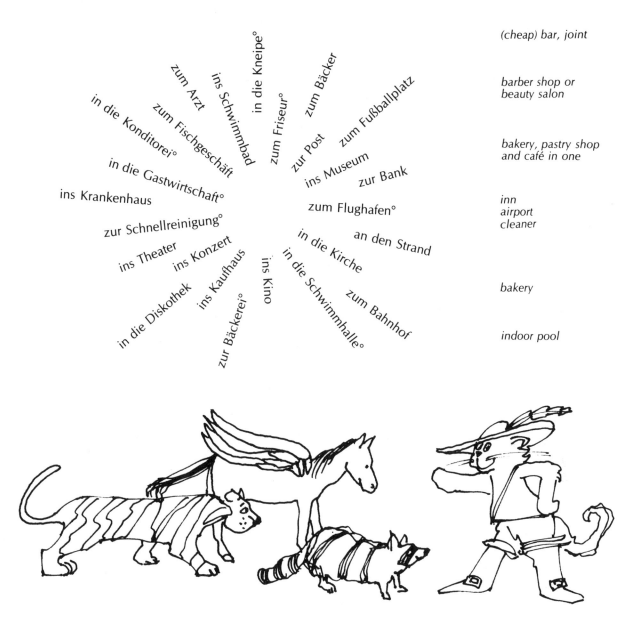

zum Bäcker

in die Kneipe°

ins Schwimmbad

zum Friseur°

zur Post

zum Fußballplatz

zum Arzt

ins Museum

zum Fischgeschäft

zur Bank

in die Konditorei°

zum Flughafen°

in die Gastwirtschaft°

ins Krankenhaus

an den Strand

zur Schnellreinigung°

in die Kirche

ins Theater

ins Konzert

zum Bahnhof

in die Diskothek

ins Kaufhaus

ins Kino

in die Schwimmhalle°

zur Bäckerei°

(cheap) bar, joint

barber shop or
beauty salon

bakery, pastry shop
and café in one

inn
airport
cleaner

bakery

indoor pool

Es gibt viele Tiere in Mythologie, Geschichte und Märchen.°
Pegasus zum Beispiel.
Pegasus ist ein Pferd mit Flügeln.° Es trägt Dichter° und ihre Gedanken.
Eine Wölfin° ernährte° Romulus und Remus, die Gründer° Roms.
Aus dem Märchen kennen wir den gestiefelten° Kater. Er ist ein kluges Tier.

fairy tale
wings
poets
she-wolf
fed, nourished
founder(s)
in boots

A KENNEN SIE TIERE AUS DER MYTHOLOGIE, dem Märchen, der Geschichte oder der Literatur?

1. Wie heißt das Tier?
2. Wie sieht es aus?
3. Was tut es?
4. Mit wem ist es zusammen?
5. Wem hilft es?
6. Wem schadet° es?
7. Andere Kommentare:

is damaging to

Amerika produziert und exportiert seine eigenen Stars unter den Tieren.

Donald Duck und Mickey Maus faszinieren Kinder und Erwachsene.

world-famous Eine Ente und eine Maus sind weltberühmt.°

Beide verdienen viel Geld. Sie sind inzwischen Millionäre.

to make [somebody] laugh and think Jeden Tag bringt der Hund Snoopy viele Menschen zum Lachen und Nachdenken.°

Garfield ist der Philosoph unter den Katzen.

 A ERZÄHLEN SIE von Donald Duck, Mickey Maus, Snoopy oder Garfield.

Wie alt ist die Frau? Schätzen Sie! _____

Warum sind der Hund und die Frau auf der Straße? _____

Wo sind Pferde gewöhnlich? _____

Wie sehen die Pferde auf dem Bild aus? _____

Was denkt der Hund? _____

Was denkt die Frau? _____

In was für einer Stadt sind wir? (deutsch, amerikanisch, alt, neu, schön, romantisch, klein, sauber, schmutzig, ...) Explain your statement.

_____

Warum sehen wir keine Autos? _____

Was denken die Leute, wenn sie die Pferde sehen? _____

Andere Kommentare und Fragen zum Bild, bitte! _____

ESSENTIAL GRAMMAR: Possessive Adjectives

Possessive adjectives are so-called **ein**—words; they take the same endings as the indefinite article **ein;** in the plural, they take the same endings as the negated indefinite article „keine."

	Singular		
	f	**m**	**n**
Nom.	**Meine Tante** heißt Bertha.	**Mein Kater** heißt Garfield.	**Mein Auto** ist kaputt.
Acc.	Ich besuche **meine Tante.**	Ich habe **meinen Kater** gern.	Ich repariere **mein Auto.**
Dat.	Ich helfe **meiner Tante.**	Ich gebe **meinem Kater** Milch.	Ich schlafe in **meinem Auto.**
Gen.	Ich spiele mit dem Hund **meiner Tante.**	Die Freundin **meines Katers** heiß Susi.	Die Tasche ist im Kofferraum **meines Autos.**

	Plural
Nom.	**Meine Freunde** studieren.
Acc.	Ich besuche **meine Freunde.**
Dat.	Ich helfe **meinen Freunden.**
Gen.	Die Eltern **meiner Freunde** sind sehr nett.

✳ **NOTE:** In contrast to English, the genitive in modern German always follows the noun it qualifies. Exception: Proper names and nouns used as such precede the noun they qualify:

Peters Tante ist sehr nett. Peter's aunt is very nice. *(No apostrophe in German.)*

Morgen ist Mutters Geburtstag. Tomorrow is Mother's birthday.

KAPITEL 6

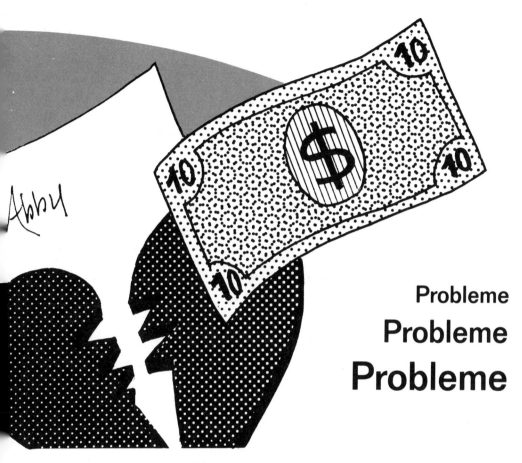

Probleme
Probleme
Probleme

Problem solving is a stimulating learning device. It probes our creative energy and imagination for a good solution. The problem of how to survive on ten dollars per week, tough as it may be for a student in real life as well as in the language classroom, can be approached and resolved in different ways: One can live on rice and milk, work in a restaurant, fast, practice meditation to reduce one's appetite, live with a friend and pool resources, live at home, join a commune, invest the ten dollars, etc. This is a fine opportunity for you to communicate freely in German—to meet the challenges of problem-solving by drawing on your own experience and to express your views in your own words.

You may want to tackle problems more "serious" than those presented in this chapter. That's fine. If you get stuck, drop the subject or try unusual solutions. The examples chosen in this chapter are intended to present a wide range of possibilities.

ERSTES PROBLEM: Babysitting

desperate calls (by phone)

Ihre Schwester, 14 Jahre alt, ist an diesem Abend Babysitterin bei Freunden. Das Baby ist ein Jahr alt. Plötzlich fängt es an zu schreien und hört nicht mehr auf. Ihre Schwester ist verzweifelt° und ruft bei Ihnen zu Hause an:° "Was soll ich tun?"

A COME UP WITH GOOD ADVICE. Counter the good advice by mentioning obstacles. Modals should prove useful, also **würde** + infinitive (**ich würde singen**—I would sing), if you are familiar with the form.

Sie sagen:	Ihre Schwester sagt:
helps, does good Du mußt das Baby aus dem Bett nehmen.	Das nützt° nichts. Es schreit noch mehr.
Maybe he (**es**) would like a bottle.	It does not want to drink.
You ought to turn on the radio.	They have no radio.
Can't you play a record?	The record player is broken.
Why don't you sing?	
You must talk with the baby.	

Why don't you give the baby
something to eat?

_____   _____

I would call the police.

_____   _____

You must not get nervous.

_____   _____

B **BRAINSTORM ABOUT BABIES IN GENERAL.** Handle it very much like the
associative chains in Kapitel 1. However, this time you should produce complete sentences.

Babys sind	
Babys haben	
Babys schreien	
Babys möchten	
Babys müssen	

ZWEITES° PROBLEM: Die Braut° sagt nein.

second
bride

Eine Braut und ihr Bräutigam° stehen vor dem Altar. Der Pastor sagt zur Braut:
"Willst du, Karola Clausen, Heinrich Berger zum Mann nehmen?"° Die Braut sagt:
"Nein!"

bridegroom
to take for a
husband

A **WHAT WOULD YOU SAY** as a non-involved observer? Among your initial reactions to such an incident might be some of the following: I find it exciting. Poor parents! That does not happen often. That's great! I would die! How can she do that? That's impossible. I would leave her. I would kill her. I like the bride.

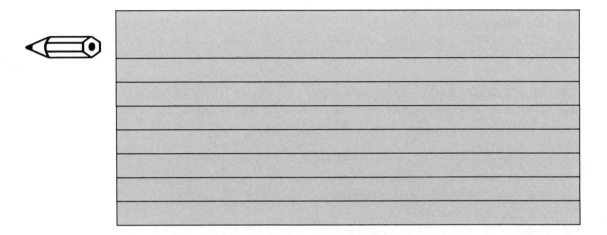

B **SIE SIND DER BRÄUTIGAM.** Was können Sie tun? Was müssen Sie tun? Was dürfen Sie nicht tun? Use the suggestions in the margin and/or your own solutions.

cry, shout, protest, run away, show her my bank account, hit her, kneel in front of her, pray, swear, embrace her, carry her away, speak to the guests, sing a song, get nervous, speak with the parents . . .

| Ich würde |
| Ich kann |
| Ich muß |
| Ich darf nicht |
| |
| |
| |
| |

C **DER PASTOR: WAS KANN ER TUN?** Was soll er tun? Was möchte er tun? Was muß er tun?

repeat the question,
talk to the bride, get
angry, go home,
send the guests
home, threaten, play
dumb and continue
the ceremony . . .

WAS KANN ER SAGEN?

What did you say?
Do you really mean
it?
Would you like a
coffee?
Did you get enough
sleep?
Shall I get a doctor?
Is that your
bridegroom?
Are you ill?
How old are you?
. . .

D Warum sagt die Braut nein? **SPECULATE** to your heart's content.

She doesn't like him.
She is afraid.
She has to think.
She finds him too
poor.
She is already
married.
She finds him too
dumb.
She wants her
freedom.
She wants to make a
scene.
She wants publicity.
She would like to
test his love.

E WAS SAGEN DIE ELTERN DER BRAUT in einer solchen Situation?

Why must this happen to us?
Karola is intelligent (emancipated, clever, etc.)
What are people going to say?
What a disappointment!

third
bursts

DRITTES° PROBLEM: Travoltas Hose platzt°

John Travolta tanzt mit seiner Partnerin Karen Gorney im New Yorker Studio 54. Das Paar tanzt ganz allein. Das Fernsehen ist da und viele Leute schauen zu. Plötzlich

seam

platzt die Naht° von Travoltas enger Hose an einer kritischen Stelle.

A WAS SOLL ER TUN? WAS KANN ER TUN?

EXAMPLE: Er soll die Tanzfläche° verlassen.°   *dance floor*
Er kann sich setzen.   *to leave*

Other options (vary **soll** and **kann:** stop, take small steps, kiss his partner, embrace Karen Gorney, attack the cameras, turn the lights off, advertise a new type of pants, invite spectators to dance, faint, lie down, dance in his underpants, . . .)

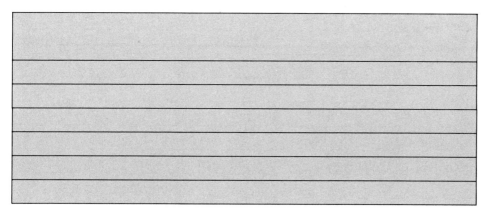

B PUT YOURSELF IN THE PLACE OF JOHN TRAVOLTA. You may have
certain intentions, polite requests, or feel certain needs.

EXAMPLE: Ich möchte mit meiner Mutter sprechen.
Ich will hier raus.
Ich muß nachdenken.°   *to think*

(vary **möchte, muß, will:** drink a whiskey, change my pants, telephone my agent, begin a new life, buy Levis, apologize to the public, cry, go to sleep, be alone, die, be at home, not give any interviews, not continue dancing, etc.)

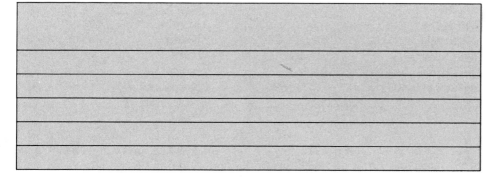

C **A PRIVATE CONVERSATION** between Karen Gorney and John Travolta after the mishap has been witnessed by millions of TV viewers and the crowd at Studio 54. Karen Gorney can be outraged, forgiving, or both. Think of their careers, friends, relatives, publicity, suggestions and plans for the future, feelings, recreating the situation, criticism of dance styles, the quality of today's clothes, observation concerning the crowd, etc.

KAREN: _____

JOHN: _____

KAREN: _____

JOHN: _____

KAREN: _____

JOHN: _____

KAREN: _____

JOHN: _____

VIERTES° PROBLEM: Romeo und Julia

fourth

Romeo möchte zu Julia. Aber das ist nicht so leicht. Er sitzt auf einer Seite des Flusses, Julia auf der anderen. Der Fluß ist etwa 20 Meter breit, 3 Meter tief, und die Strömung° ist stark. Romeo kann nicht gut schwimmen. Was Romeo und Julia vielleicht brauchen:

current

useful nouns		useful verbs	
das Boot,-e	boat	**schwimmen**	to swim
das Seil,-e	rope	**werfen**	to throw
die Brücke,-n	bridge	**bauen**	to build
der Diener,-	servant	**rufen**	to call
die Flasche,-n	bottle	**funken**	to radio
die Schwimmweste,-n	life jacket	**warten auf** (+ accusative)	to wait (for)

A **MAKE A SUGGESTION** how the problem could be solved, then let the other party reject it or find fault with it. Romeo should not be very heroic.

JULIA: Du mußt ein Boot bauen.
ROMEO: Wie soll ich ein Boot bauen? Ich habe kein Holz. Warum baust du
            nicht ein Boot?
JULIA: Mädchen bauen keine Boote. Romeo, dort ist ein Baum. Der Baum ist
            aus Holz.

ROMEO: _____

_____

JULIA: _____

_____

ROMEO: _____

_____

JULIA: _____

_____

ROMEO: _____

_____

B   WAS WISSEN SIE ÜBER SHAKESPEARES ROMEO UND SEINE JULIA?

fifth

FÜNFTES° PROBLEM: Liebe Abby!

Liebe Abby!

Ich heiße Christine. Ich habe ein Problem. Ich bin achtzehn Jahre alt und studiere Chemie an der Universität von Michigan.

Meine Mutter will, daß ich zu Hause wohne. Sie sagt:

"Du hast es gut bei uns."

"Du brauchst keine eigene Wohnung."

"Das Geld können wir sparen."

independent
rent

Ich möchte aber unabhängig° sein. Was soll ich tun? Soll ich zu Haus bleiben? Oder soll ich mir eine Wohnung mieten?°

Deine Christine

Liebe Christine!

Ich verstehe deine Situation sehr gut. Mit achtzehn möchte man unabhängig sein. Aber ich verstehe auch deine Mutter. Sie muß Essen auf den Tisch bringen, Telefonrechnungen° bezahlen, Kleidung für die Familie kaufen, usw.° Das kostet alles Geld. Ich kann Dir nicht antworten, ohne einige Fragen zu stellen:

telephone bills
etc.

1. Arbeitest Du? Wenn ja, wieviel Geld verdienst Du?
2. Kannst Du für Deine eigene Wohnung bezahlen? Wenn nein, wer soll für Deine Wohnung bezahlen?
3. Hast Du Brüder und Schwestern? Wieviele? Wo wohnen sie? Wie alt sind sie? Was machen Deine Brüder und Schwestern?
4. Wie ist Dein Verhältnis zu Deinen Eltern?
5. Hast Du zu Hause ein eigenes Zimmer?

invite

6. Darfst Du Freundinnen oder Freunde nach Hause einladen?° Wenn nicht, was sagen Deine Eltern?

idea

7. Hast Du einen festen Freund? Wenn ja, was sagt er zu Deiner Idee,° eine eigene Wohnung zu haben?
8. Was meinst Du mit "unabhängig sein?"

Herzliche Grüße,

Deine Abby

A ANSWER ABBY'S QUESTIONS by taking Christine's point of view.

B   After reviewing the evidence, **GIVE CHRISTINE YOUR ADVICE.**

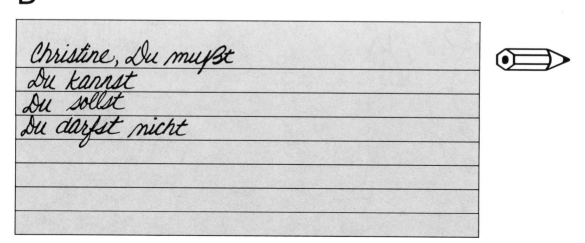

Christine, Du mußt
Du kannst
Du sollst
Du darfst nicht

C DESCRIBE YOUR OWN PROBLEM, real or invented, serious or capricious. The class, as your "Abby," will question and advise you. Be prepared to reject their advice by pointing to more problems.

TILL EULENSPIEGEL UND DER WIRT

Till Eulenspiegel can be considered the first folk hero of German literature. He died around 1350. But many stories attributed to him were invented in later centuries, a reliable indication of his popularity. He was a shrewd trickster and prankster whose activities were directed against the establishment. In this regard he is an ancestor of Wilhelm Busch's Max and Moritz, the hippies of the 1960s, the Beatles, and youthful protest against the status quo and authority in general.

freezes   Es ist Winter. Es schneit. Eulenspiegel friert.° Er sieht ein Gasthaus. Draußen ist es kalt. Drinnen ist es warm. Eulenspiegel geht hinein. Er sitzt zwei Stunden im Gast-
inn   haus,° aber er ißt und trinkt nichts. Da kommt der Wirt zu ihm und sagt: "Willst du

nichts essen und trinken?" "Nein, danke," sagt Eulenspiegel. "Du mußt aber trotzdem bezahlen," sagt der Wirt. "Seit zwei Stunden riechst du schon mein gutes Essen und sitzt in meinem warmen Gasthaus." Da lächelt Eulenspiegel und ...

A PUT YOURSELF IN EULENSPIEGEL'S PLACE and find a witty rejoinder. Check the authentic ending (printed upside down) after you have worked out your own.

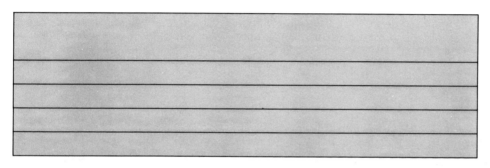

Da nimmt Eulenspiegel drei Goldstücke aus der Tasche und spielt mit ihnen vor den Augen des Wirtes. "Findest du die Goldstücke nicht wunderbar?" fragt Eulenspiegel den Wirt. "Ja," sagt der Wirt, "sie sind wunderbar. "Klingen° sie nicht herrlich?" fragt Eulenspiegel. "Ja," sagt der Wirt, "sie klingen herrlich." "Nun," sagt Eulenspiegel, "ich genieße die Wärme° deines Gasthauses und rieche dein gutes Essen. Du genießt° den Anblick° meines Geldes und seinen guten Klang.° Wir sind quitt.""

sound

warmth
enjoy
sight
sound
even

B RETELL THE STORY with your own or the authentic ending.

ESSENTIAL GRAMMAR: Modals in a Nutshell

The various problem-solving tasks of this chapter probably made you aware of how important modals are for meaningful verbal communication. The non-modified statement **Ich trinke Milch** is of rather limited functional value, unless you are responding to somebody who does not know what you are drinking or unless you express your general drinking habits or preferences. Much more often do we want to indicate intentions, likes, dislikes, or other attitudes modifying our actions. Such modifications are expressed by modals. Below is a list of German modals with their English equivalents as well as the basic attitude they convey. (German modals have infinitive forms, most English modals don't.)

Infinitive	English Equivalent	Basic Attitude
dürfen	to be allowed to, may	permission
können	to be able to, can	ability
mögen	to like to, to prefer	fondness, liking
müssen	to have to, must	compulsion, duty
sollen	ought to, to be supposed to	obligation
wollen	to want to	intention

FORMS:	dürfen	können	müssen	sollen	wollen	mögen	
ich	darf	kann	muß	soll	will	mag	möchte
du	darfst	kannst	mußt	sollst	willst	magst	möchtest
er, sie, es	darf	kann	muß	soll	will	mag	möchte
wir	dürfen	können	müssen	sollen	wollen	mögen	möchten
ihr	dürft	könnt	müßt	sollt	wollt	mögt	möchtet
sie, Sie	dürfen	können	müssen	sollen	wollen	mögen	möchten

ICH MÖCHTE—ICH MAG

Ich möchte etwas Milch trinken.
I would like to drink some milk.

Ich mag Milch.
I like milk.

Er mag Herrn Schmidt nicht.
He doesn't like Mr. Schmidt.

Frequently used equivalent:

Ich trinke gern Milch.
Ich habe Milch gern.   Er hat Herrn Schmidt nicht gern.
For all practical purposes you should learn that **möchte** expresses a polite request
and is equivalent to English "would like to." **Möchte**, like all other modals, usually
combines with an infinitive; **mag** takes a direct object.

> **NOTE!** You *must not* smoke! Du **darfst nicht** (Sie **dürfen nicht**) rauchen.

English "you must not" (in the sense of "you are not allowed to") requires a negated
form of German **dürfen**. On the other hand, **Du mußt heute nicht arbeiten** is in
English: "You don't have to work today."

MODALS WITHOUT INFINITIVES

Ich muß jetzt nach Hause. (**gehen** or **fahren** is implied)

Das darfst du nicht. (**tun** is implied)

Möchten Sie Milch? (**trinken** is implied)

When the infinitive can be inferred from the context, Germans often drop it.

 The modern day mock enmity between Prussians and Bavarians has
some historical roots, but seems to be carried out mainly for the sake of
anecdotes and jokes. The Prussian is usually featured as stiff, humorless,
bureaucratic, and formal (he usually speaks a clipped **Hochdeutsch**° in
the jokes). The Bavarian, on the other hand, is portrayed as having a
sense of boisterous, rustic humor, and being secure in his environment (he speaks his
native Bavarian dialect). He usually comes out on top.

Ein Bayer° sitzt im Hofbräuhaus° neben einem Preußen.°

"Mein Herr," sagt der Preuße zum Bayern, "Sie sitzen auf meinem Hut!"

"Na, und?" sagt der Bayer. "Wollen Sie schon gehen?"

standard German (as opposed to dialects or slang)

*Bavarian
famous beerhall in Munich
Prussian*

KAPITEL 7

Superman

& Siegfried

In an age of mass media, TV and movies have become a major source for communication between individuals. Complete strangers sitting next to each other on a plane can immediately engage in a lively discussion of a TV series or a recent film. As language learners we should make use of such shared experience. We share stories supported by memories of images that do not need any introduction. The story of a TV episode or movie is a sequence of events structured enough to provide continuity and direction for our communication, but not too rigid to stop communication if certain information is omitted. Since a movie usually appeals to us rationally and emotionally, our motivation to provide, extract, and analyze information should be very high. Retracing the events of a film will activate a wealth of ''useful'' vocabulary.

SUPERMANN

Gestern bin ich mit meiner Freundin ins Kino gegangen.

Wir haben *Supermann* gesehen.

leading role   Christopher Reeve hat die Hauptrolle° gespielt.

Der Film hat uns sehr gefallen.

Die Geschichte hat auf dem Planeten Krypton begonnen.

Der Planet war in Gefahr zu explodieren.

Supermanns Eltern haben ihren Sohn—er ist noch ein Baby—in eine Raumkapsel gesetzt.

Sie haben die Raumkapsel in den Weltraum geschossen, um ihren Sohn zu retten.

Dann ist der Planet Krypton explodiert.

space   Supermann ist als Baby durch den Weltraum° geflogen.

older   Er ist während dieser Zeit älter° geworden.

Die Kapsel ist irgendwo in Dakota gelandet.

Das Supermann-Baby ist aus der Kapsel gestiegen.

Es hat noch seine Windeln angehabt.

Ein Bauer hat den kleinen Supermann gefunden.

Er und seine Frau haben das Baby adoptiert.

Schon als Kind hat Supermann seine Kraft gezeigt.

Einmal hat sein Adoptivvater sein Auto repariert.

jack (for raising a car)   Da ist der Wagenheber° umgefallen°.

fell over, collapsed   Aber Supermann hat den Wagen mit seinen Händen gestützt.°

supported

So hat er seinem Adoptivvater das Leben gerettet.
In der Schule ist Supermann im Sport der Beste° gewesen.
Er hat einen Fußball aus dem Stadion geschossen.
Er hat einen Zug überholt.°   *overtook (passed)*
Nach der Schule ist er nach New York gegangen.
In New York ist er Reporter geworden.
Er hat für *The Daily Planet* gearbeitet.
Aber nach der Arbeit ist er Supermann gewesen.
Er hat ein Mädchen kennengelernt.
Er ist mit ihr ausgegangen und ausgeflogen.

A **ERZÄHLEN SIE MEHR** von Supermann. Sie können *Supermann I, Supermann II* oder *Supermann III* benutzen.

_____

_____

_____

_____

B **PUT IT TOGETHER.** One half of the class reads the cues to the other half which should supply the complete sentence. Switch roles after six cues.

... ins Kino gegangen.
... gesehen.

... die Hauptrolle gespielt.

... uns sehr gefallen.

... Planeten Krypton begonnen.

... war in Gefahr zu ...

... in eine Raumkapsel gesetzt.

... in den Weltraum geschossen, um ...

... explodiert.

... durch den Weltraum geflogen.

... älter geworden.

... gelandet.

... aus der Kapsel gestiegen.

... Windeln angehabt.

... Supermann gefunden.

... adoptiert.

... seine Kraft gezeigt.

... repariert.

... umgefallen.

... mit seinen Händen gestützt.

... das Leben gerettet.

... der Beste gewesen.

... aus dem Stadion geschossen.

... überholt.

... nach New York gegangen.

... Reporter geworden.

... gearbeitet.

... kennengelernt.

... ausgegangen und ausgeflogen.

C FIND OUT ABOUT FILMS that your classmates have seen by asking some of the following questions. Prepare your own answers in the space provided.

1. Welchen Film hast du gesehen?

_____

2. Wer hat die Hauptrolle gespielt?

_____

3. Was war der Held von Beruf?

_____

4. Wie hat er ausgesehen?

_____

5. Was waren seine Hobbys?

_____

6. Was waren seine Stärken?°   _strengths_

_____

7. Was waren seine Schwächen?°   _weaknesses_

_____

8. Wo hat die Geschichte gespielt?

_____

9. Wie hat der Film begonnen?

_____

10. Wer hat wen geliebt?

_____

11. Wer hat wen geheiratet?

_____

12. Wer hat wen gehaßt? Warum?

_____

13. Wer hat wen getötet?° Warum?   _killed_

_____

14. Wie ist der Film weitergegangen?° Was ist dann passiert? Was hat der Held°   _went on, did go on_
    (die Heldin) dann gemacht?   _hero_

_____

15. Wie war das Ende des Films?

_____

16. Hat es ein Happy End gegeben?

_____

17. Erzählen Sie eine besonders interessante Szene aus dem Film.

_____

_____

_____

_____

D CREATE YOUR OWN FILM STORIES. Use the clues to get you started.

1. In meinem Film spielt Burt Reynolds einen _____.

   Er _____.

   In meinem Film explodiert kein Planet, sondern _____.

   Die Leute _____.

2. Dolly Parton heiratet in meinem Film _____.

   Dolly Parton und _____.

3. Mein neuer Film heißt *Superman X.*
   Bei mir kommt Supermann nicht von dem Planeten Krypton, sondern er

   _____. Als Baby fliegt Supermann _____ und

   _____ und _____.

made a movie

spy
Russia

4. Ich habe einen Film mit Clint Eastwood gedreht.° Clint Eastwood ist ein ameri-

   kanischer Spion.° Er fliegt nach Rußland° und _____

   _____.

actress

5. Ich halte Meryl Streep für eine sehr gute Schauspielerin.° Mein neuester Film

   heißt _____.
   Meryl Streep spielt eine Professorin. Sie liebt einen Studenten. Der Student

   _____. Meryl Streep _____.

king
photographer
mistake

6. In meinem neuen Film spielen Woody Allen und ich die Hauptrollen. Ich bin der
   König° von Schweden (die Königin von England). Woody Allen ist Photograph.°
   Als Photograph macht er viele Fehler.° Er hat keinen Film in der Kamera. Der

   König (die Königin) sagt: ''_____.''
   Er will den König (Königin) photographieren und fällt ins Wasser. Der König (Die

   Königin) sagt: ''_____.''

revenge
death

SIEGFRIED—LIEBE, RACHE° und TOD°

Greeks

Fast alle Völker haben einen starken Mann in ihrer mythischen Geschichte. Die
Griechen° haben Herkules, die Spanier haben den Cid, die Amerikaner haben
Supermann, und die Deutschen haben Siegfried.

Kennen Sie Siegfried? Früher hießen viele deutsche Jungen und Männer Siegfried, besonders unter Hitler. (Warum wohl?)

Wie wurde Siegfried so berühmt? Zunächst° besiegte° er einen Drachen.° (Auch Herkules, der heilige Georg und andere Helden mußten Drachen besiegen.) Dann badete Siegfried im Blut des Drachen und bekam davon eine Hornhaut.° Die Hornhaut machte ihn unverwundbar°—nur an einer Stelle zwischen den Schultern nicht. Siegfried hatte auch eine Tarnkappe.° Mit der Tarnkappe konnte er sich unsichtbar° machen. Seine Kraft, sein Schwert° und seine Tarnkappe machten Siegfried zu einem ausgezeichneten° Kämpfer.° Er half den Königen von Burgund°—drei Brüdern—bei ihren Kriegen. Ein Grund für seine Hilfe war Kriemhild, die Schwester der Könige. Sie war sehr schön, und Siegfried liebte sie sehr. Aber Siegfried durfte Kriemhild noch nicht heiraten. Denn die Könige brauchten noch einmal seine Hilfe. Gunther wollte eine Frau heiraten, die eigentlich viel zu stark für ihn war. Sie hieß Brunhild und wohnte auf einer einsamen° Insel.° Wer sie heiraten wollte, mußte ein guter Sportler° sein. Er mußte sie im Weitsprung,° im Kugelstoßen° und im Speerwerfen° besiegen. Das konnte Gunther natürlich nicht. Und wieder mußte Siegfried helfen. Unter seiner Tarnkappe warf Siegfried den Speer für Gunther, stieß die Kugel

first
defeated
dragon
callus
invulnerable
cloak of invisibility
invisible
sword
excellent
fighter
Burgundy

lonesome, remote
island
athlete
long jump
shot put
throwing the javelin

für Gunther und sprang für ihn. So besiegte "Gunther-Siegfried" die starke Brunhild und nahm sie mit nach Worms. Das war damals die Hauptstadt° von Burgund. In

capital (city)

splendid
double wedding

Worms gab es dann eine prachtvolle° Doppelhochzeit:° Gunther heiratete Brunhild, und Siegfried heiratete Kriemhild.

Nun denken Sie: "Die Geschichte hat ein Happy-End. Alle sind glücklich." Das stimmt aber leider nicht. In der Hochzeitsnacht hielt Brunhild ihren schwachen Mann zum Narren.° Sie fesselte° ihn an Händen und Füßen und hängte ihn zum Spaß an einen Nagel.° Gunther mußte Siegfried noch einmal um Hilfe bitten, und Siegfried half ihm natürlich.

made fun of
tied
nail

showed off, bragged

Langsam merkte Brunhild, was hier los war. Außerdem prahlte° Kriemhild auch noch mit ihrem starken Siegfried. So wurde Brunhild böse und wollte Rache.

Eines Tages kamen Siegfried und Kriemhild nach Worms zu Besuch. Die Frauen sprachen über dieses und jenes; die Männer wollten jagen. Sie wissen: Siegfried war durch das Blut des Drachen unverwundbar—nur an einer Stelle zwischen den Schultern nicht. Beim Bad im Drachenblut war ein Lindenblatt° zwischen seine Schultern gefallen. Brunhild bat Hagen, einen Freund ihres Mannes, Siegfried zu töten.° Auch Hagen haßte Siegfried und war deswegen° gern zum Mord° bereit.° In Amerika würden wir heute sagen: Hagen wurde Brunhilds "hitman."

leaf from a linden
tree
to kill
therefore
murder
ready

protect
cross
vulnerable

"Ich bin Siegfrieds Freund," sagte Hagen zu Kriemhild. "Ich möchte ihn bei der Jagd beschützen.° Nähe ihm ein Kreuz° auf sein Hemd genau an der Stelle, wo er verwundbar° ist! Dann kann ich ihn besser beschützen." Kriemhild liebte ihren Mann sehr und tat es.

Vielleicht kennen sie das Ende. Bei der Jagd wurde Siegfried durstig und wollte an einer Quelle° trinken. Da traf Hagen ihn mit einem Speer genau an der Stelle, wo *well, spring* das Kreuz war. So starb Siegfried.

Männliche Chauvinisten werden sagen: ''Hier sehen wir es wieder einmal. Die Frauen sind an allem schuld;° erst Samson und Delilah, dann Helena und der *are to blame* Trojanische Krieg, nun Brunhild. Und Kriemhilds Rache° ist eine andere Geschichte. *revenge*

A **DESCRIBE SIEGFRIED, GUNTHER, BRUNHILD.** Use information from the text. You may add your own perceptions and judgments. Use the past tense.

1. Siegfried war ein starker Mann.

   Siegfried _____ (vulnerable)

   Siegfried _____ (Kriemhild)

   Siegfried _____ (die Könige von Burgund)

   Siegfried _____ (Gunther)

2. Gunther war kein starker Mann.

Er _____ (Brunhild)

Er _____ (needed Siegfried)

Er _____ (im Speerwerfen, Weitsprung, Kugelstoßen)

Gunther _____ (exploited Siegfried)

Gunther _____ (had two brothers)

3. Brunhild _____ (strong)

Brunhild _____ (Gunther)

Brunhild _____ (Hagen)

B Wer ist schuld an Siegfrieds Tod? **LOOK INTO THE ACTIONS** of each individual person that imply more or less serious guilt.

1. Hagen _____

2. Brunhild _____

3. Kriemhild _____

4. Gunther _____

5. Siegfried _____

C Sie haben eine Tarnkappe wie Siegfried. **WAS WÜRDEN SIE TUN?**

EXAMPLE: Ich würde Fort Knox besuchen.
Ich würde drei Tage in einer Bank bleiben.

eat every day in expensive restaurants, fly to Europe every weekend, watch Queen Elizabeth at breakfast, irritate Johnny Carson, destroy all rockets, play with lions …

Ich würde

_____

_____

_____

_____

D BRUNHILD DEFENDS HER ACTIONS.

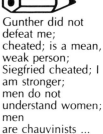

Gunther did not defeat me; cheated; is a mean, weak person; Siegfried cheated; I am stronger; men do not understand women; men are chauvinists ...

E RETRACE THE TALE with the help of the following cues. If some of the cues lead you to digressions, digress and return to the story when running out of material.

Mythos vom starken Mann	Worms
die Griechen	Doppelhochzeit
die Spanier	Happy-End
Siegfried	hielt zum Narren
besonders unter Hitler	an einen Nagel
einen Drachen	um Hilfe bitten
Hornhaut	Brunhild merkte
an einer Stelle nicht	Kriemhild prahlte
eine Tarnkappe	zu Besuch
den Königen von Burgund	jagen
Kriemhild	unverwundbar
durfte noch nicht heiraten	ein Lindenblatt
Gunther wollte eine Frau heiraten, die	Brunhild ... Hagen
wohnte auf	Hagen ... Siegfried
ein guter Sportler	beschützen
warf für Gunther	ein Kreuz
sprang	bei der Jagd
stieß	aus einer Quelle
"Gunther-Siegfried"	mit einem Speer

ESSENTIAL GRAMMAR: The Present Perfect and the Past

PRESENT PERFECT: CHARACTERISTICS AND USAGE COMPARED TO THE PAST

In German, the Present Perfect (**das Perfekt**) is crucial for talking about events in the past. The Present Perfect has an immediacy and liveliness that is characteristic of events recalled from the recent past. For instance, you would use the Present Perfect when talking to your parents about your day after returning from school or work, or when retelling the storyline of a film you saw last night (compare the account of *Supermann* in this chapter). You can give the same immediacy to events that are normally narrated in the Past (such as events in novels, fairy tales, and history books), if you want to convey a sense of excitement, or immediacy, or personal involvement to a listener. For instance, fairy tales are usually written in the past, and you read them to children in the past. But if you told the same fairy tale without the help of the written text, you would naturally slip into the Present Perfect whenever you wanted to dramatize certain particularly captivating events.

PRESENT PERFECT: FORMATION OF THE PRESENT PERFECT, ARTICLES AND THE USE OF *HABEN* UND *SEIN* AS AUXILIARIES

EXAMPLES:
1. Ich **habe** ihm die Stadt **gezeigt**.
2. Er **hat** heute schwer **gearbeitet**.
3. Peter **ist** nach New York **gefahren**.
4. Meine Tante **ist** sehr alt **geworden**.
5. Wir **sind** gerade aus Deutschland **zurückgekommen**.
6. Schumanns **haben** ihr Haus **verkauft**.
7. Meine Freundin **hat** in Berlin **studiert**.
8. Wir wissen, daß er seine Frau sehr **geliebt hat**.

ANALYSIS: (Numbers in parentheses refer to the examples)
a. The Present Perfect is usually formed with a form of **haben** + past participle (1, 2, 6, 7, 8).
b. The Present Perfect is formed with a form of **sein** + participle, if the verb indicates a change of place (3) or change in condition (4).

In addition, **bleiben, geschehen, passieren** *(to happen)*, **gelingen** *(to succeed)*, and **sein** require a form of **sein** + participle to form the Present Perfect.

c. Regular or weak verbs form the participle with the prefix **ge-** + stem + **t** (1) or **et**, if the stem of the verb ends in **t** or **d** (2).

d. Irregular or strong verbs form the participle with the prefix **ge-** + stem + **en** (2, 4, 5). (Most strong verbs undergo a vowel change in the past participle.)

e. The past participle of separable verbs (for instance, **zurückkommen**) is formed by combining the separable prefix and the past participle, for example: **zurückgekommen** (5).

f. No **ge-** is required to form the participles of verbs with inseparable prefixes, for example: **verkauft** (6). The most common inseparable prefixes are **be-, emp-, ent-, er-, ge-, ver-,** and **zer-.**

g. No **ge-** is required to form participles of verbs whose infinitive ends in **-ieren,** for example: **studiert** (8).

h. In main clauses, the participle goes to the end of the clause (1-7). In a subordinate clause, the participle immediately precedes the conjugated verb (8).

THE PAST TENSE: CHARACTERISTICS AND USAGE COMPARED TO THE PRESENT PERFECT

The Past Tense can be considered characteristic of novels, stories, fairy tales, historical accounts and similar narratives (our story of Siegfried, for instance). It is more the tense of writing than speaking about events in the past. If the Present Perfect signals immediacy and liveliness, the Past Tense reflects a certain detachment.

THE PAST TENSE: FORMS

Weak Verbs	Strong Verbs	Modals
ich kaufte	ich fuhr	ich konnte
du kauftest	du fuhrst	du konntest
er	er	er
sie kaufte	sie fuhr	sie konnte
es	es	es
wir kauften	wir fuhren	wir konnten
ihr kauftet	ihr fuhrt	ihr konntet
sie Sie kauften	sie Sie fuhren	sie Sie konnten

REMARKS: 1. The **-t-** is the signal for the past tense of weak verbs and of modals.

2. Modals drop the umlaut in the past tense.

3. Strong verbs change stem vowel. No endings in the first and third persons singular.

haben	**sein**	**werden**
ich hatte	ich war	ich wurde
du hattest	du warst	du wurdest
er	er	er
sie hatte	sie war	sie wurde
es	es	es
wir hatten	wir waren	wir wurden
ihr hattet	ihr wart	ihr wurdet
sie hatten	sie waren	sie wurden
Sie	Sie	Sie

fights

A Auf diesem Bild kämpft° Siegfried mit dem Drachen. **HAT SIEGFRIED EINE CHANCE?** Warum? Warum nicht?

_____

_____

_____

Warum kämpft Siegfried gegen den Drachen? _____

_____

B Siegfried braucht guten Rat in dieser Situation. **GEBEN SIE IHM GUTEN RAT!**

Siegfried, du mußt
Du darfst nicht
Du sollst
Ich würde
Vielleicht kann Supermann

C SIEGFRIED, VICTORIOUS, IS TELLING HIS ADVENTURE to a group of
friends. Let him talk about the size of the dragon, its looks, how long it took to
defeat it, what he thought before and during the fight, who or what helped him, what
he did after the fight, etc. Siegfried may brag.

smith

tongs, pliers
anvil

Auch Siegfried muß lernen. Auf diesem Bild lernt er bei einem Schmied.° Heute gibt es kaum noch Schmiede. Diese Arbeit machen heute Bethlehem Steel in Amerika und die Firma Krupp in Deutschland. Siegfried schlägt das heiße Eisen mit einem Hammer, der Meister hält das Eisen mit einer Zange,° das Eisen liegt auf einem Amboß.°

MÖCHTEN SIE BEI DIESEM MEISTER LERNEN? Warum? Warum nicht?

_____

_____

_____

Was denkt Siegfried? _____

Was denkt der Mann in der Mitte° mit der Zange? _____   _middle_

Was denkt der Meister? _____

BIN DER GRÖSSTE!

Bragging is a favorite pastime of children. It is a spontaneous, emotionally charged, and creative activity. Its adult equivalent can often be found in advertising, resumés, and job interviews.

ANGEBEN

Muhammad Ali is no longer "The Champ," but his boxing skills, his success, his antics, and especially his uninhibited theatrical bragging have created a myth that will endure. The bragging match between Muhammad Ali and Joe Frazier actually took place. But the German version presented here is an attempt to capture the spirit of the match rather than a literal translation. It is strongly recommended for imitation and variation.

Muhammad Ali	**Joe Frazier**
Ich bin der Größte!	Du bist der Größte? Da muß ich aber lachen! Deine Klappe° ist sicher größer als meine. Aber ich boxe besser.
Besser als ich? Da muß ich aber lachen. Joe, ich glaube, du träumst.° Besser als ich? Ich bin schneller als du, schlage härter als du. Und ich bin auch viel intelligenter als du.	
	So, so! Wo war deine Intelligenz in New York? Da hast du klar gegen mich verloren.
Das war Zufall.° Du hattest viel Glück! Ich steche wie eine Biene° und gleite° wie ein Schmetterling.	Ich soll vor einer Biene Angst haben? Da muß ich aber lachen. Übrigens sind Schmetterlinge sehr schlechte Flieger.°
Mein lieber Joe, ich glaube, du bist neidisch.° Du weißt, ich bin der schönste Mann im Ring. Vielleicht sogar der schönste Mann auf der ganzen Welt.	
	Du bist ein grosser Schauspieler!° Lieber Ali! Warum gehst du nicht nach Hollywood? Jetzt bist du noch schön. Nach dem nächsten Kampf mit mir ist deine Nase platt° wie eine Briefmarke.
Wer hat die größere Klappe, ich oder du? Du redest zuviel,° lieber Joe. Reden° ist Silber, Schweigen° ist Gold.	Du redest wie eine alte Frau, Ali. Du erinnerst mich an meine Oma,° Ali. Du gehörst in ein Altersheim.° Und bald brauchst du ein Gebiß.°
Du redest wie ein Baby, Joe. Ich glaube, du brauchst einen Schnuller.° Du mußt jeden Tag viel Milch trinken. Dann wirst du groß und stark. Wer möchte gegen ein Baby kämpfen?	

Marginal glosses:

"trap" (slang for mouth)

dream

coincidence, luck, chance
bee
glide

flier
envious

actor

flat, flattened

too much talking
keeping silent
granny
nursing home, home for the aged
false teeth
pacifier

Lassen Sie Ali
sprechen! Er hat
viel zu sagen.

A **PREPARE FOR A VARIATION** of the Ali-Frazier "Battle of the Mouths" by making lists of brief corresponding statements you might want to use. Don't feel hampered by fragmentary information about Ali and Frazier. This is the time for bragging!

	Ali	**Frazier**
	Ich bin der Größte!	
		Ich bin der Stärkste.
	Ich bin jünger als du.	
experience		Ich habe mehr Erfahrung° als du.
	Ich steche wie eine Biene.	
lion		Ich kämpfe wie ein Löwe.°

_____

_____

_____

_____

_____

_____

_____

_____

_____

_____

B For presentation in class, **HAVE A CLASSMATE CUE YOU** with Ali's lines (You should know your own lines by heart). Switch roles.

VERKAUF UND REKLAME

Selling a product is an everyday situation in most cultures and has probably reached a high point in western, especially American civilization. Billboards scream messages, advertisement reaches us from the pages of newspapers and magazines, from the TV screen, and through the hyped-up voices of radio announcers. Sometimes we are annoyed by it, sometimes amused. Selling a product lends itself to exaggeration. Make fun of advertising and enjoy doing it. The topic chosen as an example is intentionally far-out to indicate the total range of this task. You can remain much more realistic and still be humorous with your sales pitch!

Sind Sie immer müde?

Haben Sie Probleme mit Ihren Kursen an der Uni?

Bekommen Sie immer Cs und Ds?

Dann ist es höchste Zeit° für "Intelligenz-Extra."   *high time*

"Intelligenz-Extra" ist die Antwort, die einzige Antwort, die ganze Antwort.

"Intelligenz-Extra" löst° Ihre Probleme effektiv, individuell und diskret.   *solves*

"Intelligenz-Extra" wirkt sofort und ist dabei garantiert° unschädlich.°   *guaranteed*
harmless

Eine Pille "Intelligenz-Extra" am Morgen, und Ihr Intelligenzquotient schießt° in die Höhe: bis 170 und höher.   *shoots up*

"Intelligenz-Extra" macht Sie frisch, aktiv und kreativ.

Mit "Intelligenz-Extra" sind Sie der Konkurrenz immer um einen Schritt voraus:

> Sie lernen schneller als andere Studenten.
>
> Sie behalten° mehr als andere Studenten.   *retain (remember)*
>
> Sie wissen mehr als die Professoren.
>
> Sie funktionieren so präzis wie ein Computer.
>
> Im Denken der Originellste, im Schreiben der Schnellste.
>
> Im Leben der Erfolgreichste.°   *most successful*

"Intelligenz-Extra"—der schnellste, sicherste Weg zum Erfolg!

A **QUESTION THIS SALES EFFORT.** Ask questions about price, people who have taken this product, what happens if you take two pills per day, what about competition if all the students take it, why do they have to advertise if "Intelligenz-Extra" is so good, ask if the advertising person has taken it, if there is a difference between men and women taking it, how does it become effective, etc. Two groups should handle questions and answers.

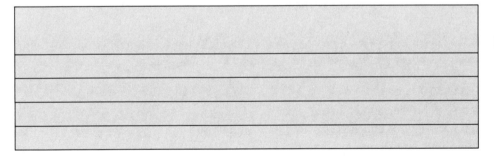

B **MAKE YOUR OWN SALES PITCH** for a. a new economy car, b. a new beer, c. a multi-purpose kitchen utensil (use drawing), d. an object of your own choice. Stay close to the sequence and syntax of the sentences used in the example.

This will ensure correct sentence structure and make it easier for your classmates to understand your sales pitch.

EXAMPLES: Sind Sie immer müde?
Haben Sie Probleme mit Ihren Kursen an der Uni?
Ist Ihr Auto oft kaputt?
Haben Sie Probleme mit Ihren Bremsen?

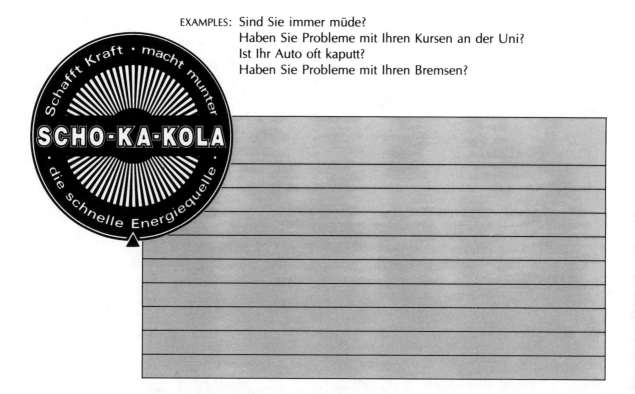

DIE TRAUMKANDIDATIN

dream candidate (female)

Writing a resumé is a more conventional, subtle form of bragging. Here is your chance to beat all contenders for a position:

Ich bin 19 Jahre alt.

Ich spreche vier Sprachen.

Ich habe Physik und Betriebswirtschaft° studiert.

business, management (as a field of study)

Mein Intelligenzquotient liegt bei 160.

Mein Vater war ein guter Bekannter von Albert Einstein.

Im letzten Jahr war ich Miss Ohio.

advertisement Im Fernsehen mache ich Reklame° für Revlon.

acting lessons Ich spiele Gitarre und nehme Schauspielunterricht.°

A MAKE UP ADDITIONAL QUALIFICATIONS.

B QUESTION INDIVIDUAL ITEMS OF THE RESUMÉ: raise doubts about her age (she might look older or younger), question her language proficiency, ask her how and where she got her degrees, etc.

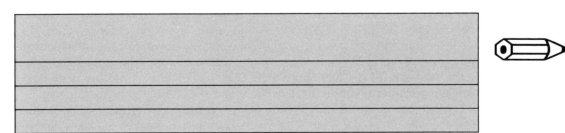

C **WRITE A RESUMÉ** that is sure to land you a job in one of these fields. You may brag and stun: a. a stuntman, b. a cook, c. a clown, d. a diplomat, e. a model, f. an astronaut.

REKORDE, REKORDE, REKORDE...

Höher, weiter, stärker, schneller—das ist das Motto der Olympischen Spiele. 1983 lief Calvin Smith 100 Meter in 9,93 Sekunden. Das sind 22,53 Meilen pro Stunde. Calvin Smith ist der schnellste Mann der Welt. Er ist elfmal schneller als ein Faultier (zwei Meilen pro Stunde), dreimal schneller als eine Schlange (sieben Meilen pro Stunde) und fast zweimal schneller als (oder: fast doppelt° so schnell wie) ein Schwein (13 Meilen pro Stunde). Aber Calvin Smith ist zweimal langsamer als (oder: doppelt so langsam wie) ein Windhund° (46 Meilen pro Stunde), fast dreimal langsamer als eine Antilope (61 Meilen pro Stunde) und fast fünfmal langsamer als eine Schwalbe,° das schnellste Tier der Welt (100 Meilen pro Stunde).

1976 gewann Bruce Jenner bei den Olympischen Spielen in Montreal die Goldmedaille im Zehnkampf.° Später machte er im Fernsehen Reklame° für "Wheaties." Essen Sie genug "Wheaties," und auch Sie können Olympiasieger im Zehnkampf werden! Cassius Clay *alias* Muhammad Ali wurde 1960 Olympiasieger im Schwergewicht.° Dann wurde er Profi,° Weltmeister° im Schwergewicht und sehr reich. Muhammad Ali liebt Superlative. Er ist natürlich nicht nur der beste Boxer, sondern auch der schönste, intelligenteste und populärste Mann aller Zeiten.

Möchten Sie auch einmal Weltmeister werden? Das ist leichter, als Sie glauben. Das *Guinness Buch der Weltrekorde* wird Ihnen helfen. Kennen Sie die schwersten

double

greyhound

swallow

decathlon
advertisement

heavyweight
a professional (in sports)
world champion

Zwillinge° der Welt? Sie heißen Benny und Billy McCrary. Sie kommen aus Hender- *twins*
sonville, North Carolina und wogen 1978 zusammen fast 1500 Pfund: Billy wog
743, Benny 723 Pfund.

    Es ist nicht einfach, so schwer wie Billy und Benny zu werden. Versuchen Sie
etwas Leichteres. Vielleicht können Sie Weltmeister im Lachen, Weltmeister im
Sitzen, Weltmeister im Eisessen oder Weltmeister im Kaugummikauen° werden. Sie *chewing chewing*
müssen nur ein Gebiet finden, auf dem Sie wirklich gut sind und keine oder wenig *gum*
Konkurrenz° haben. *competition*

A Quiz: Fakten. **ANSWER ORALLY IN COMPLETE SENTENCES.** If in doubt,
consult your teacher or friends.

1. Was ist höher: das Empire State Building in New York oder der Sears Tower in Chikago?
2. Welcher Staat hat die meisten Einwohner: New York, Texas oder Kalifornien?
3. Was ist härter: Stahl oder Diamant?
4. Wo ist es kälter: am Nordpol oder am Südpol?
5. Was ist teurer: Gold oder Silber?
6. Welcher Staat ist größer: Oregon oder Connecticut?
7. Wer läuft schneller: Calvin Smith oder ein Windhund?
8. Was ist länger: ein Kilometer oder eine Meile?
9. Welcher Tag ist der längste Tag des Jahres?
10. Welcher Tag ist der kürzeste Tag des Jahres?

B Quiz: Persönlicher Geschmack. **ANSWER IN COMPLETE SENTENCES.**

1. Was trinken Sie gern?
2. Was trinken Sie lieber: Kaffee oder Tee?
3. Was trinken Sie am liebsten: Kaffee, Tee, Milch, Wein, Bier, Orangensaft° oder *orange juice* etwas anderes?
4. Essen Sie mehr zum Frühstück als zum Mittagessen?
5. Was mögen Sie weniger gern: Froschschenkel° oder Sauerkraut? *frog legs*
6. Was schmeckt Ihnen besser: Sauerbraten oder Wiener Schnitzel?
7. Gehen Sie öfter ins Kino als ins Theater?
8. Interessiert Sie Musik mehr als Literatur?
9. Was gefällt Ihnen besser: Jazz oder klassische Musik?
10. Finden Sie Fußball interessanter als Tennis?

Was schmeckt besser? Ein Hamburger von Burger King oder ...?
Was ist am teuersten?

11. Arbeiten Sie am Morgen intensiver als am Abend?

12. Wissen Sie mehr über Autos als über Politik?

ideas
library
somewhere else

13. Wann oder wo bekommen Sie die besten Ideen:° in der Bibliothek,° beim Autofahren, im Schlaf, im Garten, beim Kaffeetrinken, im Kino oder sonstwo?°

future

14. Wovor haben Sie am meisten Angst: vor Schlangen, vor Prüfungen, vor dem Altwerden oder vor der Zukunft?°

C **MOST SUPERLATIVES ARE HIGHLY SUBJECTIVE AND UNFAIR,** because they exclude so much. **INDULGE ANYWAY,** because your verdict will provoke others to state their own opinions. Try to give a reason for your statement.

EXAMPLE: Wo ist es am ruhigsten? In der Bibliothek ist es am ruhigsten. Kein Radio spielt.

Wo ist es am teuersten

am schönsten

am gemütlichsten

am lautesten

am langweiligsten

am gefährlichsten

am sichersten

am interessantesten

auf Hawaii, am Nordpol, in der U-Bahn, auf dem Mount Everest, in der

Diskothek, in der Konditorei, in der Vorlesung,° an der Universität, unter Wasser, *lecture*

am Strand,° bei Hardees, beim Friseur,° in der Badewanne, im Konzert, bei uns, *beach*
barber (hair stylist)

auf einem Baum, im Bett, am Meer, zwischen zwei Kobras, bei der Polizei, im

Gefängnis° *prison*

D MAKE COMPARISONS, use **singen** and **spielen**.

EXAMPLE: Louis Armstrong singt tiefer als Barbra Streisand.

lauter als
genauso laut wie
höher als
genauso sentimental wie
schlechter als
genauso schlecht wie
besser als
erfolgreicher° als *more successful*
verrückter als
konzentrierter als
genauso elegant wie

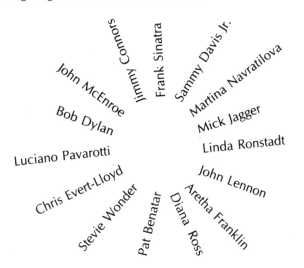

John McEnroe
Jimmy Connors
Frank Sinatra
Sammy Davis Jr.
Martina Navratilova
Bob Dylan
Mick Jagger
Luciano Pavarotti
Linda Ronstadt
Chris Evert-Lloyd
John Lennon
Stevie Wonder
Pat Benatar
Diana Ross
Aretha Franklin

E BEI DEN OLYMPISCHEN SPIELEN

gibt es viele Rekorde. Warum?
sieht man Menschen aus der ganzen Welt. Warum?
hat das Fernsehen viel zu tun. Warum?
sitzen viele Zuschauer im Stadion. Welche Probleme gibt es?
gibt es leider auch Nationalismus. Geben Sie Beispiele!
verdienen manche Leute viel Geld. Wer? Wie?
hört die Politik nicht auf. Geben Sie Beispiele!
hat die Polizei viel zu tun. Warum?

F **TALK ABOUT THE OLYMPIC GAMES** in Los Angeles. You may want to put some of the statements under E in the past tense and add your own.

Bei den Olympischen Spielen in Los Angeles

G **EIN SPORTLER WIE CARL LEWIS** muß viel trainieren. Was darf er/darf er nicht? Was muß er/darf er nicht? Was will er/will er nicht? Was soll er, kann er/kann er nicht, möchte er/möchte er nicht? (Some negations will have to be produced with "kein(e).")

drugs
advertisement

gesund essen
Alkohol trinken
rauchen
viel trainieren
jeden Abend ausgehen
Fußball spielen
durch die ganze Welt reisen
Konkurrenz haben

Drogen° nehmen
Reklame° machen
Präsident werden
Interviews geben
Filme machen
mit 60 Jahren Weltmeister werden
jeden Tag Pizza essen

sailing
cycling

H Bruce Jenner machte Reklame für "Wheaties." **SIE SIND OLYMPIASIEGER** in einer dieser Sportarten: im Boxen, im Marathonlauf, im Reiten, im Segeln,° im Skilaufen, im Schießen, im Radfahren,° über 100 Meter. **JETZT MACHEN SIE REKLAME.** (Remember that Olympic champions not only advertise for a product they use, but for things that seem to be supported or enhanced by their discipline.)

EXAMPLE: Ich bin Olympiasieger im Marathonlauf.
Ich mache Reklame für Vitamine. Der Tag ist lang. Sie brauchen Vitamine.

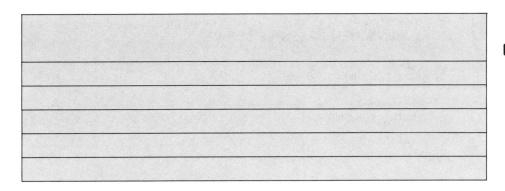

SIE MÖCHTEN IN DAS *GUINNESS BUCH DER WELTREKORDE* KOMMEN. Auf welchem Gebiet möchten Sie Weltmeister werden? Wie trainieren Sie dafür? Some possibilities: Weltmeister im Biertrinken, im Duschen, im Pizzaessen, im Kaugummikauen.°

chewing chewing gum

EXAMPLE: Ich möchte Weltmeister im Lachen werden. Ich lese jeden Tag *Mad Magazine* und studiere bei Johnny Carson.

Was braucht ein Weltmeister im Burgenbauen? Wie trainiert er? Stellen Sie Fragen an einen Weltmeister im Burgenbauen!

J Billy McCrary wog 743 Pfund. Das kann problematisch werden.
DICKE MENSCHEN HABEN ES SCHWER,

Kleidung zu kaufen. Warum?

_____

Arbeit zu bekommen. Warum?

_____

*go in for sport, to be
an athlete*

Sport zu treiben.° Warum?

_____

im Auto zu sitzen. Warum?

_____

K **ALTE MENSCHEN**

sind oft allein. Warum?

_____

brauchen Hilfe. Geben Sie Beispiele.

_____

möchten bei ihren Kindern wohnen. Stimmt das? Warum? Warum nicht?

_____

haben viel gesehen. Was hat eine achtzigjährige Amerikanerin z. B.
gesehen?

_____

können gut erzählen. Wovon erzählen Sie?

_____

haben oft wenig Geld. Was ist das Resultat?

_____

müssen öfter als junge Menschen zum Arzt gehen. Warum?

_____

reisen gern. Warum?

_____

möchten gern noch etwas im Haushalt helfen. Wobei?

_____

sind Menschen zweiter Klasse. Stimmt das?

_____

Was machen alte
Menschen gern?
Was sagen alte
Menschen oft über
junge Menschen?

L WAS WERDEN SIE TUN, WENN SIE ALT SIND?

EXAMPLE: Ich werde viel lesen.

Ich werde _____

learn to swim.

_____

marry.

sleep late.

write a book.

play with my grandchildren.

_____

visit the moon.

_____

not live in Florida.

_____

go out every night.

_____

count my money.

_____

play cards with my friends.

_____

advertise "Wheaties."

_____

sit in the sun.

_____

drink a glass of wine every day.

_____

make my neighbors angry.

ESSENTIAL GRAMMAR: Making Comparisons

Positive	**Comparative**	**Superlative**
1. Foreman ist schnell.	Frazier ist schneller.	Ali ist am schnellsten.
2. Foreman boxt intelligent.	Frazier boxt intelligenter.	Ali boxt am intelligentesten.
3. Der VW ist ein schnelles Auto.	Der Mercedes ist ein schnelleres Auto.	Der Porsche ist das schnellste Auto.
4. Mein Freund boxt *so gut wie* du.	5. Ich boxe *besser als* er.	

Unlike English (compare cheap, cheaper, cheapest and beautiful, more beautiful, most beautiful), German has only one way of comparing adjectives and adverbs: **-er** is added in the comparative, **-(e)st** in the superlative.

The formation of positive, comparative, and superlative is alike for adjectives and adverbs. (see examples 1, 2).

The superlative of predicate adjectives and adverbs always appears in the form of **am ... sten: am schnellsten, am intelligentesten** (see examples 1, 2).

When used in an attributive function (examples 3), the comparative and superlative forms of the adjective require appropriate endings just like an adjective in the positive.

Most monosyllabic adjectives add an umlaut to their comparative and superlative forms:

jung	jünger	jüngst-
alt	älter	ältest-
groß	größer	größt-

When the stem of the superlative ends in **d, t, s, ß,** or **z,** an **e** is slipped in between stem and **st** to facilitate pronunciation:

intelligent	intelligent*est*-
süß	süß*est*-

Some of the most frequently used adjectives and adverbs have irregular comparative and superlative forms and should be memorized:

gern	lieber	liebst-
gut	besser	best-
hoch (hoh-)*	höher	höchst-
nah(e)	näher	nächst-
oft	öfter	meist-
viel	mehr	meist-

Inequality is expressed by comparative + **als** (example 5).
Equality is expressed by **so** + positive + **wie** (example 4).

> ✳ NOTE: **genauso schön wie** just as beautiful as
> **nicht so schön wie** not as beautiful as

*hoch is the predicate form, hoh- is the stem of the attributive form:
  Dieser Baum ist dreißig Meter hoch.
  Das ist ein hoher Baum.

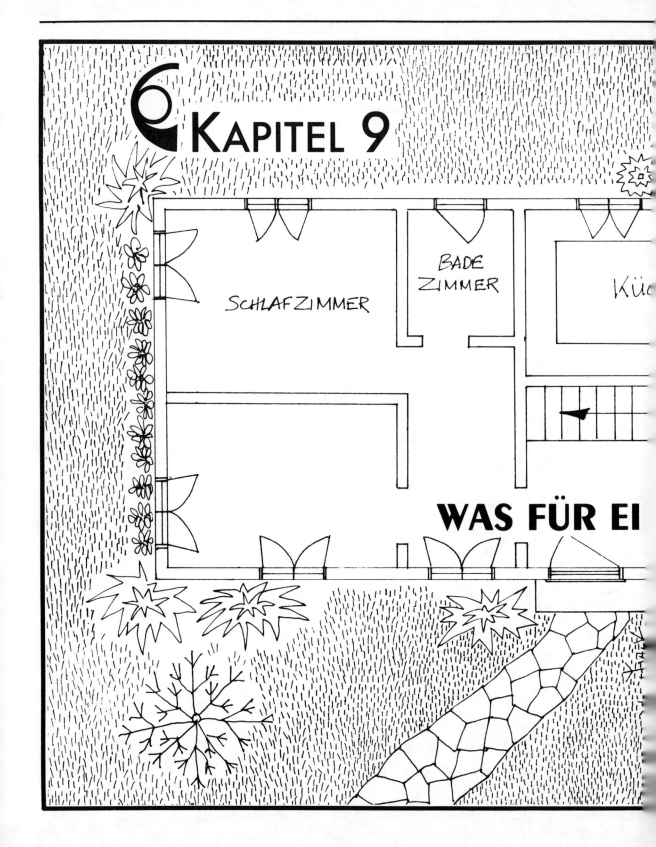

KAPITEL 9

SCHLAFZIMMER

BADE ZIMMER

Kü

WAS FÜR EI

ESSZIMMER

TERRASSE

AUS! WAS FÜR EINE FAMILIE!

Pictures provide a welcome change of pace in any language class. The eye is given something to relate to, to explore, and hopefully to enjoy. You no longer have to rely exclusively on your memory to produce foreign words and sentences. You can name and comment on visible persons, objects, activities, and relationships. Yet, pictures suggest much more than they show. Even the most primitive drawing will trigger a wealth of associations which may produce more language activity than a teacher's most thoughtful questions. Make use of this treasure of memories; speculate about the motives, thoughts and plans behind the scenes and characters. In fact, the descriptive aspect of the picture, although supplying you with raw material, should become secondary. The fun begins when your imagination becomes active and produces language.

WAS FÜR EIN HAUS! WAS FÜR EINE FAMILIE!

A **REACT TO THE PICTURE.** Comment upon anything anywhere in the picture, unrestricted by the teacher's directions. Any form of utterance is equally welcome: statements, questions, exclamations, and even meaningful fragments of sentences. This period should be limited to about five minutes. Write down some of the comments that you particularly liked, would like to come back to, or found noteworthy in some other respect.

bathroom,
spiders
millipede, centipede

EXAMPLE: Die Frau ist sehr groß.
Regnet es im Badezimmer?°
Spinnen° und Tausendfüßler!°
Wer ist der Mann im Sessel?

B **STATE WHAT YOU SEE,** like, dislike, or question in the basement:

Ich sehe   .

Man erkennt   .

Ich mag die Maus. Sie ist   .

Ich mag   nicht.

Ich hasse   .

Das Fahrrad sieht   aus.

Der Junge sieht   aus.

C Der Junge mit dem Lasso heißt Ottokar. Er ist das "schwarze Schaf" der Familie. Er ist 9 Jahre alt. **WARUM SPIELT OTTOKAR WOHL IM KELLER?**

EXAMPLE: Ottokar spielt im Keller, weil es ihm Spaß macht.

weil _____ .

the cat is in the basement.

weil _____ .

he wants to play with the cat.

weil _____ .

the basement is more interesting than the children's room.

_____ .

_____ .

_____ .

_____ .

_____ .

D **GLAUBEN SIE, DASS OTTOKAR DEN KATER FÄNGT?**

EXAMPLE: Ottokar fängt den Kater, wenn der Kater dumm ist.

wenn _____ .

if the cat does not jump.

wenn _____ .

if the cat likes water.

wenn _____ .

if Bodo's water pistol does not function.

_____ .

_____ .

_____ .

_____ .

squirts

E Der Junge mit der Wasserpistole hinter den Weinflaschen heißt Bodo. Bodo ist Ottokars Bruder. Er ist 7 Jahre alt. **WARUM SPRITZT° BODO MIT DER WASSERPISTOLE?**

EXAMPLE: Bodo spritzt, damit Ottokar den Kater° nicht fängt.   *tomcat*

damit _____.
the cat does not catch the mouse.
damit _____.
Ottokar gets angry.
damit _____.
the cat gets a chance.

_____.

_____.

_____.

Bodo spritzt den Kater, um Ottokar zu ärgern.°   *annoy*

um _____.
in order to irritate the cat.
um _____.
in order to test the water pistol.
um _____.
in order to save the mouse.
um _____.
in order to help the mouse.

_____.

_____.

_____.

F KETTENREAKTION: EINS FÜHRT ZUM ANDEREN.

Als Ottokar den Kater sah, holte er sein Lasso.
Als Ottokar sein Lasso holte, kam die Maus aus dem Loch.

Als die Maus aus dem Loch kam, _____.
the cat wanted to catch the mouse.

Als _____, _____.
Ottokar threw the lasso.

Als _____, _____.
Bodo squirted the cat.

Als _____,   _____.
                                                     the cat jumped on the wine bottles.

Als _____,   _____.

Als _____,   _____.

Als _____,   _____.

Als _____,   _____.

Als _____,   _____.

Think of bottles being broken, Mr. Schmidt hearing the noise, Mr. Schmidt getting up, coming down the stairs, shouting, Ottokar hiding, Bodo getting punished, Bodo screaming, etc. "Kettenreaktion" works best with voluntary contributions from the class or alternating between two groups.

G **SPECULATE ABOUT MR. SCHMIDT.** He is the man sitting in the chair watching TV. Use his environment, events in the house (real and imagined), as well as your own personal opinion. Consider the topics listed in the margin.

his age, time of the day, his physical and mental condition, type of work, attitude toward family, interests, vacation plans, political views, taste, etc.

H **FRAU SCHMIDT IST TRAURIG. WARUM?**

Sie weiß, daß ihr Mann schon wieder fernsieht.

daß _____.
he drinks too much.

daß Ottokar _____.

daß Klaus und Günther _____.

Sie hofft, daß _____.

Sie wünscht, daß _____.

Sie fürchtet, daß _____.

Sie möchte, daß _____.

Sie freut sich, daß _____.

Was soll Frau Schmidt tun, damit sie bessere Laune bekommt?

Sie soll ins Kino gehen.

Sie soll _____.

Sie muß _____.

Sie muß vielleicht _____.

Sie darf nicht _____.

Sie kann _____.

Sie könnte _____.

Sie kann vielleicht _____.

Kinder spielen gern im
Badezimmer, weil ...
Fragen Sie den Jungen: Was
...? Wie lange ...? Warum
...?

| **MAKE LISTS OF POSSIBLE ACTIVITIES** suggested by some of the rooms.

Im Badezimmer:

to fight
to shave
to brush one's teeth
to sing
to comb one's hair

Im Keller:

to throw the lasso
to sled
to ski
to come down the stairs
to hide
to clean

Im Kinderzimmer:

Ich sehe ... Das ist ... Was liegt ...? Was steht ...? Was sagen Eltern oft über Kinder und Kinderzimmer?

J "60 MINUTES" COMES TO THE SCHMIDT HOME.

Wir möchten wissen, warum Herr Schmidt soviel trinkt.

wie _____ .

wo _____ .

Ein Mann aus Ohio fragt, ob _____ .

Unser Publikum möchte wissen, welche Platten° _____ .

Können Sie uns sagen, Herr Schmidt, _____ .

Mike Wallace weiß nicht genau, _____ .

Haben Sie schon gehört, daß _____ .

Wußten Sie schon, daß _____ .

SUPPLY ANSWERS to the questions. **PRODUCE MORE QUESTIONS** and have them answered.

K Ulrike (mit Zigarette) und Sabine sind schon junge Damen. Ulrike ist 16, Sabine ist 15. **LASSEN SIE ULRIKE UND SABINE ERZÄHLEN:** was sie so am Tag machen, was in der Schule los ist,° wie sie mit ihrer Familie auskommen° (Ottokar!!), was für Hobbys sie haben, usw. Das Bild soll Ihnen helfen. Stellen Sie z.B. Beziehungen her:

is going on
get along

millipede, centipede

records

Ottokar
rauchen
Günther
Tausendfüßler°

Ulrike   Schallplatten°   Sabine   Fledermaus°

Vater
Hund
Mutter
Schule

L Der Boden hat viele Möglichkeiten. Was kann man aus dem Boden machen? Was würden Sie aus dem Boden machen? **BESCHREIBEN SIE IHRE PLÄNE GENAU!**

DEUTSCHE SCHIMPFWÖRTER

ONE-WORD INSULTS

German	Literal Translation	Equivalent
Angsthase!	timid hare	"chicken"
Blödmann!	stupid man	"moron"
Dummkopf!	stupid head	"stupid"
Feigling!	coward	coward
Frosch!	frog	"chicken" (timid person)
Flasche!	bottle	poor performer (sports)
Idiot!	idiot	idiot
Klugscheißer!	clever shitter	know-it-all
Niete!	lottery blank	"loser"
Schlauberger!	Mr. Clever	wise guy

Usually the one-word insult is preceded (and often) followed by "du." **Du Angsthase, du!**

EXPRESSIONS FOR CRAZINESS

Du hast einen Knall.	You have an explosion.	You're crazy.
Du hast einen Vogel.	You got a bird up there.	You're crazy.
Bei dir piept's wohl.	You got something chirping up there.	You're crazy.
Du hast zu heiß gebadet	The bath you took was too hot, i.e. heat affected your brain.	You're crazy.
Bei dir ist eine Schraube locker.	You got a screw loose, i.e. don't function.	You're crazy.
Du spinnst!	You are spinning yarn.	You're crazy. You must be kidding.
Du hast nicht alle Tassen im Schrank.	You don't have all your cups in the cupboard.	You don't have all your marbles.

EXPRESSIONS FOR STUPIDITY:

Dumm bleibt dumm, da helfen keine Pillen

Du geistiger
Tiefflieger, du!
Dumm wie
Bohnenstroh!
Du denkst so weit,
wie eine fette Sau
springt!

You intellectual
strafer (low flier).
As stupid as
beanstraw.

A MUDSLINGING. Point out to each other how stupid, crazy and cowardly you are. Don't limit yourself to the German insults given in the catalog. (By the way, if you work in groups, you will have to use the plural forms of those insults). The following examples and English cues are intended to inspire your production of insults:

Du Blödmann, du weißt nicht, was 1 + 1 ist.
Ihr Dummköpfe, ihr wißt nicht, wer Einstein war.
Ihr Idioten, ihr könnt nicht bis drei zählen.
Ihr wißt nicht, wo New York liegt.
Ihr wißt nicht, wir Ihr heißt.
Ihr wißt nicht, warum Ihr zur Universität geht.
Ihr wißt nicht, daß die Erde rund ist.
Ihr eßt einen Apfel und sagt: "Die Orange schmeckt gut."
Ihr möchtet auf der Autobahn schlafen.
Ihr macht nie den Mund auf.

stupidity

B DUMMHEIT°

1. Ihr wißt nicht, was 1 + 1 ist.
   Ihr wißt nicht, was _____ .

(what an apple is, what people in Detroit produce, what Colonel Sanders sells, what Charles Lindbergh did, what a teacher, a doctor, a busdriver, Muhammad Ali, etc. does, what your telephone number is, what Germans like to drink, what Americans like to eat, what cats like to catch, what a baby needs, what fish need, what Americans chew, what Germans wear, what "Guten Tag" means, what a nuclear bomb can do)

2. Ihr wißt nicht, wo New York liegt.

wo _____.

(where your head is, where people build cars, where one can eat, where people make films, where your parents live, where Superman landed [worked, played football, saved his father, met a girl], where you can read books, study, dance, etc.)

3. Ihr wißt nicht, warum ihr zur Universität geht.

warum _____.

(why you buy cigarettes, why you leave the door open, why people have to work , why a car needs gasoline, why it rains, why it is cold in the winter, why you went to see a doctor, why you flew to Germany, why you hate your uncle, why you got up this morning, why you want to watch TV, etc.)

4. Ihr wißt nicht, wie ihr heißt.

wie man _____.

(how to drive [one drives] a car, how to turn on the light, how to open a bottle, how to get into a car, how to say hello, how to read, how to order a beer, etc.)

5. Ihr wißt nicht, daß die Erde rund ist.

daß _____.

(that a week has seven days, that today is your birthday, that Paris is a city in France, that people have been on the moon, that Shakespeare wrote *Romeo and Juliet*, that you came without pants, that you have sold your house, etc.)

6. Ihr könnt nicht bis drei zählen.

Ihr könnt nicht _____.

(read, add, multiply, divide, say hello, drive a car, write a letter, count your money, make a telephone call, etc.)

7. Ihr seid zu dumm, um bis drei zu zählen.

um _____.

(to read a newspaper, to buy bread, to look out of the window, to drink from [aus] a glass, to order breakfast, etc.)

C VERRÜCKTHEIT.° The borderline between stupidity and ignorance on the one hand and craziness on the other is subjective and fluid. Let us attribute the following activities to craziness:

craziness

Ihr eßt einen Apfel and sagt: "Die Orange schmeckt gut."

_____ .

You visit Johnny Carson and say: "Hello, Mr. Reagan."

_____ .

You drink a glass of beer and say: "This wine is unusual."

_____ .

You take a trip to Alaska in order to waterski.

_____ .

You get into your car and say: "When does the bus leave?"

_____ .

You are in your friend's kitchen and say: "What a beautiful bathroom."

_____ .

You meet Tarzan and say: "You chicken!"

_____ .

You jump from the Empire State Building.

_____ .

You would like to sleep on the Autobahn.

_____ .

You try to count every tree in the United States.

_____ .

You find the nuclear bomb harmless.

cowardice

D **FEIGHEIT.**° Again, a very subjective and biased judgment. Kapitel 2 has some examples that you may want to consult in addition to the following suggestions and your own insults.

Ihr macht nie den Mund auf.

Ihr _____ .
       always say "yes."

_____ .
are afraid to cross the street.

(never take a plane, never take a boat, never swim in the ocean, never try something new, always stay at home, never play tennis, never eat in a restaurant, don't leave the house in the winter, always ask your father and mother, write letters to "Dear Abby," etc.)

DIE GESCHICHTE VON ISIDOR
(Nach einer Episode in Max Frischs Roman "Stiller")

Isidor war Apotheker (wahrscheinlich in einer kleinen Stadt in der Schweiz°). Er verdiente gut, hatte fünf Kinder und führte, wie man so sagt, eine glückliche Ehe°. Nur eines konnte er nicht vertragen:° wenn seine Frau ihn fragte: "Wo bist du denn wieder gewesen, Isidor?" Und das fragte sie oft. Obwohl er dann innerlich° sehr böse° war, zeigte er es äußerlich° nie. Denn er war, wie man so sagt, ein guter Ehemann.°

    Auf einer Reise nach Mallorca, einer spanischen Touristeninsel° im Mittelmeer,° kam Isidor mit seiner Frau zunächst° nach Marseille. Von dort wollten sie dann mit dem Schiff nach Mallorca weiterfahren. Während seine Frau schon auf dem Schiff nach Mallorca stand, ging Isidor noch einmal an Land, um eine französische° Zeitung zu kaufen. Auf die Frage seiner Frau, "Wohin gehst du denn, Isidor?" gab er natürlich keine Antwort. So passierte es, daß das Schiff mit seiner Frau nach Mallorca

Switzerland
marriage
tolerate, endure,
"stand"
inside
angry
on the outside
husband
tourist island
the Mediterranean
at first

French

freighter
foreign legionaries

homeland
returned
birthday
beard
sun helmet
belt
recognized
Daddy
sunshade
wonderful
birthday cake
embrace
foreign legion
had spent
whipped cream
spattered
mess
robe
was spattered
put
put on

fuhr. Isidor dagegen finden wir auf einem schmutzigen Frachter,° der einige hundert Fremdenlegionäre° nach Nordafrika brachte. Wie Isidor auf diesen Frachter gekommen ist, weiß niemand. (Haben Sie eine Theorie?)

Die Fremdenlegion machte Isidor, wie man so sagt, zum Mann. Nach Hause schreiben durfte er nicht. So vergaß Isidor langsam seine Apotheke, seine Frau und sogar seine Heimat° (die Schweiz). Nach sieben Jahren kehrte° er am Geburtstag° seiner Frau nach Hause zurück.° Denn Isidor war immer noch ein guter Ehemann. Obwohl er jetzt einen Bart° hatte, einen Tropenhelm° trug und einen Revolver am Gürtel,° erkannten° ihn seine Kinder sofort und schrien: "Der Papi, der Papi!"° Seine Frau saß auf der Terrasse unter einem Sonnenschirm,° die wunderbare° Geburtstagstorte° vor sich auf dem Tisch. Isidor, der seine Frau sieben Jahre nicht gesehen hatte, wollte sie umarmen.° Da sagte sie: "Isidor, wo bist du denn so lange gewesen?"

Das war zuviel für einen Mann, der sieben harte Jahre in der Fremdenlegion° verbracht hatte.° Isidor zog den Revolver und schoß dreimal in die schöne Geburtstagstorte. Die Schlagsahne° spritzte° nach allen Seiten. Das war eine schöne Schweinerei.° "Also Isidor!" sagte seine Frau, deren Morgenrock° über und über mit Schlagsahne bespritzt war°. Isidor steckte° in aller Ruhe seinen Revolver in den Gürtel, setzte° seinen Tropenhelm auf° und ging.

A The joys, hazards, advantages, drawbacks and other characteristics of certain occupations and professions. **USE THE CUES AND ADD YOUR OWN OBSERVATIONS:**

Apotheker verdienen   .
Apotheker   .
Mein Arzt sagt immer, daß
(length of studies, hard work, white coats, much on TV)
Stewardessen reisen viel, aber
Stewardessen   .
Als Bäcker würde ich
Lehrer wissen

List more professions/occupations and their characteristics.

_____

_____

_____

B Sie sind Vater oder Mutter von fünf Kindern: Bodo, Ottokar, Sabine, Ulrike und Klaus. **SHOW HOW USEFUL IT IS TO HAVE FIVE CHILDREN.** Assign chores to each of your "children" by pointing at fellow students in class. Be tough! In return, the smart child should have a good excuse. Check the list of "attractive" chores.

EXAMPLE: Bodo, du mußt abwaschen.
Tut mir leid. Ich muß Englisch lernen.

_____   _____

_____   _____

_____   _____

_____   _____

A list of "attractive" chores:

aufräumen	to clear up, tidy, put things in order	
abwaschen°	to do the dishes	_do the dishes_
einkaufen gehen	to go shopping	
Zigaretten holen	to go and get cigarettes	
den Wagen waschen	to wash the car	
Schnee schaufeln	to shovel snow	
den Hund ausführen	to go for a walk with the dog	
den Keller saubermachen	to clean the basement	
die Betten machen	to make the beds	
auf die Kinder aufpassen	to watch the children, to babysit	
Kaffee kochen	to make coffee	
staubsaugen	to vacuum	

C **DESCRIBE AN UNHAPPY MARRIAGE** which linguistically is probably more interesting than a happy one. Let us call the husband Isidor and his wife Isolde.

Isidor und Isolde sprechen nicht miteinander.°   _with each other_
Isidor hat zwei Freundinnen.
Isolde kocht...

_____.

_____.

_____.

_____.

D SIE MACHEN EINE REISE nach a. Rußland, b. Hawaii, c. Deutschland, d. zum Mond.

arise

Was nehmen Sie mit?
Was wollen Sie dort tun?
Welche Probleme können entstehen?°
Was bringen Sie als Souvenir mit nach Hause?

> EXAMPLE: Rußland

Ich nehme meinen Wintermantel mit.
Ich möchte das Bolschoi Ballett sehen.
Vielleicht darf unser Flugzeug nicht landen.
Ich bringe eine Flasche Wodka mit nach Hause.

_____ .
_____ .
_____ .
_____ .

E WIR WISSEN NICHT, WIR VERSTEHEN NICHT, WIR KÖNNEN NICHT SAGEN.

freighter

> EXAMPLE: Wie Isidor auf den Frachter° gekommen ist, wissen wir nicht.

Swiss

Was Herr Reagan	, verstehe ich nicht.
Warum meine Freundin	, sage ich nicht.
Wieviel ein Bernhardiner	, wissen nur die Schweizer.°
Wo Dan Rather	, habe ich nicht erfahren.
Wofür die Amerikaner	, wissen nur die Götter.
	.
	.

F WIE IST ISIDOR AUF DEN FRACHTER GEKOMMEN?
(the French made him drunk, he did not want to travel with his wife, he hated Mallorca, he was nosy and curious, he wanted adventure, he saw a friend on the freighter, he found Switzerland boring, he wanted to talk with the captain, wanted a free trip to Africa, etc.)

G Indulge in clichés once again. **LIST SOME TYPICAL, PREDICTABLE QUESTIONS.**

Mein Vater fragt immer: _____?

_____?

_____?

Meine Mutter fragt immer: _____?

Meine Freundin fragt immer: _____?

Mein Chef fragt immer: _____?

Mein Mann fragt immer: _____?

Meine Frau fragt immer: _____?

H You have been away from home for seven years. **REPORT ON YOUR ARRIVAL AT HOME.**

Als ich nach Hause kam, saß mein Vater im Sessel und sah fern.

_____

_____

_____

I **CHANGE THE SCENE OF ISIDOR'S RETURN.**

Als Isidor nach Hause kam, war seine Frau verreist.°
               wurden seine Kinder böse.°

on a trip
angry

_____

_____

_____

J FIND A DIFFERENT ENDING FOR THE STORY.

ESSENTIAL GRAMMAR: Subordinate Clauses

squirts
had laid the table

goes out

yelling, hollering

1. Bodo spritzt° mit der Wasserpistole, damit Ottokar den Kater nicht fängt.
2. Nachdem Frau Schmidt den Tisch gedeckt hatte,° rief sie die Kinder.
3. Ottokar spielt im Keller, weil er den Kater fangen will.
4. Wir hoffen, daß Herr Schmidt manchmal mit seiner Frau ausgeht.°
5. Ich weiß nicht, ob Frau Schmidt am Nachmittag spazierengehen möchte.
6. Als Herr Schmidt nach Hause kam, hörte er lautes Geschrei° im Badezimmer.
7. Wir möchten wissen, warum Herr Schmidt so viel trinkt.
8. Ottokar ist der "junge Mann," der die Familie tyrannisiert.

Although subordinate clauses are grammatically complete sentences, they cannot stand by themselves, as main clauses can. They need a main clause (preceding or following) in order to convey complete, logical meaning.

A subordinate clause may be introduced by a subordinating conjunction such as **als, damit, daß, weil,** etc. (1-6), an interrogative such as **warum, wie, wo, was,** etc. introducing an indirect question (7), or a relative pronoun such as **der, die, das** or their equivalents **welcher, welche, welches** (8).

For all practical purposes you should learn that the subordinating conjunction is immediately followed by the subject of the subordinating clause.

For most learners of German, the end position of the conjugated verb (full verb, auxiliary, or modal) is the most puzzling characteristic of a German subordinate clause. Especially in spoken German, waiting for the verb to appear can be tantalizing.

Infinitives and participles immediately precede the conjugated verb (2, 3, 5).

The separable element of a separable verb is reconnected with the conjugated verb (4), participle, or infinitive (5).

Subordinate clauses may precede main clauses (2, 6); this causes the word order in the main clause to be inverted (the subject of the main clause follows immediately behind the verb (6 . . ., hörte er . . .).

KAPITEL 10

John Travolta

Conducting an imaginary interview with a show business celebrity is a worthwhile language class activity. You are probably familiar with such celebrities and their work, idiosyncracies, the gossip surrounding them, etc. Usually there is an emotional relationship between you and such celebrities, such as admiration, affection, or dislike. These act as natural stimulants for questions. If conducted in a spirit of playfulness almost any question is possible and meaningful. The invented interview with John Travolta is intended to show you useful speech patterns, especially questions, and the possible spirit of such an interview.

INTERVIEW WITH JOHN TRAVOLTA

REPORTER: Herr Travolta, tanzen Sie gern?

TRAVOLTA: Das ist eine dumme Frage. Natürlich tanze ich gern. Haben Sie nicht meinen Film "Saturday Night Fever" gesehen?

REPORTER: Sie tragen phantastische Hemden. Wo kaufen Sie Ihre Hemden?

give, present

TRAVOLTA: Ich kaufe mir keine Hemden. Meine Freundinnen schenken° sie mir.

REPORTER: Man sagt, Sie haben viele Freundinnen. Wieviele Freundinnen haben Sie?

TRAVOLTA: Das weiß ich nicht. Ich habe sie nicht gezählt.

REPORTER: Was sagt Ihre Mutter dazu?

TRAVOLTA: Sie sagt: "Junge, du mußt wissen, was du tust."

REPORTER: Wie oft gehen Sie aus?

twice
That really depends.

TRAVOLTA: Ein- oder zweimal° pro Woche. Das kommt ganz darauf an.°

REPORTER: Wohin gehen Sie meistens?

TRAVOLTA: Ich gehe meistens ins Studio 54. Dort treffe ich viele Freunde aus Hollywood.

REPORTER: Was für einen Wagen fahren Sie?

TRAVOLTA: Ich fahre einen Alfa Romeo.

REPORTER: Travolta ist ein italienischer Name. Stammt Ihre Familie aus Italien?

comes from
Ireland

TRAVOLTA: Ja, die Familie meines Vaters stammt° aus Italien, die Familie meiner Mutter aus Irland.°

relations, ties with

REPORTER: Haben Sie Beziehungen° zur Mafia?

TRAVOLTA: Glauben Sie alles, was in der Zeitung steht?

revealing,
informative
my pleasure
It was a pleasure.
again
cordial

REPORTER: Ich danke Ihnen für das aufschlußreiche° Interview.

TRAVOLTA: Bitte sehr, gern geschehen.° Es war mir ein Vergnügen.°

REPORTER: Auf Wiedersehen. Und nochmals:° vielen herzlichen° Dank.

A COME UP WITH ALTERNATIVES for question 1: "Herr Travolta, tanzen Sie gern?"

Herr Travolta, boxen Sie gern?

Herr Travolta, _____?
    do you like to flirt

_____?
    do you like to protest

_____?
    do you like to read

Herr Travolta, gehen Sie gern aus?

Herr Travolta, _____ ?

do you like to watch TV

_____ ?

do you like to take a walk

_____ ?

do you like to play cards

_____ ?

do you like to drink wine

_____ ?

do you like to swim

_____ ?

do you like to go to the movies

_____ ?

do you like to stay home

_____ ?

do you like to ride a bicycle

_____ ?

do you like to go skiing

B Since we are playing a game, occasional rude or far-out answers should be welcome. Answers of this kind help to create a humorous context, keep the questioner alert, and teach you an important principle of foreign language learning: never say "I can't say it." Say it differently, say something else that is close, talk your way out of a difficulty. This attitude keeps you flexible, inventive and leads to the discovery of other words and phrases in context. **TRY A VARIETY OF ANSWERS** to the reporter's second question, "Wo kaufen Sie Ihre Hemden?" Take a few cues in English and then make up your own answers.

_____ .

I buy them in the supermarket.

_____ .

I don't wear shirts.

_____ .

I don't have any money.

I buy them where they are cheap.
Can you recommend a store?
That is a private matter.
That is none of your business.

C **PRETEND YOU ARE TRAVOLTA'S MOTHER** and come up with statements that center around the following aspects: that John is drinking too much, that he does not send home any money, that he is getting older, that he hates women, that he learned dancing from her, that he is a horrible pilot, that she wants 13 grandchildren, that John is married, but does not tell anybody, etc.

D Explore potential question-and-answer situations that are indicated in the diagram.

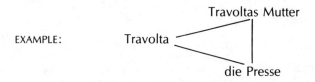

EXAMPLE:

DIE PRESSE: Frau Travolta, wie war John als Kind?
FRAU TRAVOLTA: John war ein gutes Kind.
JOHN TRAVOLTA: Nein, das stimmt nicht,° ich war kein gutes Kind. Ich habe *That's not true.*
meiner Mutter nicht geholfen. Ich habe meine Schwester
geärgert.° *annoyed, teased*
FRAU TRAVOLTA: Glauben Sie ihm nicht. Seine Schwestern haben ihn geärgert.
DIE PRESSE: Wie alt sind Ihre Schwestern?

JOHN TRAVOLTA: Meine älteste Schwester ist _____.
DIE PRESSE: Wo wohnt Ihre Schwester?

JOHN TRAVOLTA: Meine Schwester wohnt _____.

DIE PRESSE: _____.

JOHN TRAVOLTA: _____.

FRAU TRAVOLTA: _____.

Now try other combinations:

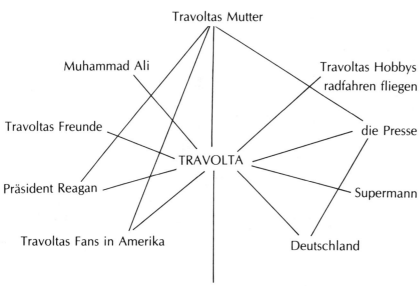

E TALK ABOUT THE ADVANTAGES AND DISADVANTAGES OF LIFE IN HOLLYWOOD as you perceive it by forming two groups, one pro, one con, alternating the statements. Think of smog, sun, too many people, mild winter, ocean, beach, noise, always something going on, lack of privacy, contrast between rich and poor, etc.

pro	contra
Das Wetter ist schön.	Die Luft ist schlecht.
Man hat gute Chancen.	Das Leben ist dort zu teuer.
_____	_____
You meet famous people.	*There is too much crime.*
_____	_____
You may see many beautiful girls.	*You get frustrated.*
_____	_____
A film director may discover you.	*Everybody talks about movies.*

Warum lächeln die jungen Damen?
Sechs junge Damen—sechs Wünsche für die Zukunft. „Ich möchte ..." In Hollywood ...

_____ .   _____ .

_____ .   _____ .

_____ .   _____ .

_____ .   _____ .

F **CHARACTERIZE A CELEBRITY.** Use the characterization of John Travolta as a model.

John Travolta	Miss Piggy
Er sieht gut aus.	_____
Er ist groß.	_____
Er verdient viel Geld.	_____
Er ißt gern Spaghetti.	_____
Er hat viele Freunde.	_____
Er kann gut tanzen.	_____
Er hat viele Filme gemacht.	_____
Er fährt einen Alfa Romeo.	_____
Seine Mutter liebt ihn.	_____

_____   _____

_____   _____

G **INTERVIEW PRESIDENT REAGAN,** Brooke Shields, Miss Piggy, or any other celebrity of your choice by using the Travolta interview as a pattern. It can be quite productive to retain questions that appear to be inappropriate for a person. Asking Miss Piggy, "Haben Sie Beziehungen zur Mafia?" seems to be strange, but could lead to an interesting answer.

REPORTER: _____

_____ : _____

REPORTER: _____

_____ : _____

REPORTER: _____

dream
steep
career

EIN AMERIKANISCHER TRAUM°—JOHN TRAVOLTAS STEILE° KARRIERE°

leaves
high school
actor
lugs
boxes

Mit sechzehn verläßt° er die Oberschule° in Englewood, New Jersey, weil er Schauspieler° werden will. Im Supermarkt schleppt° er Kisten° für fünfundzwanzig Dollar pro Woche. Und weil Fliegen sein Traum ist, nimmt er Flugstunden: für fünfundzwanzig Dollar pro Stunde.

Mit einundzwanzig spielt er Vinnie Barbarino in der Fernsehserie "Welcome Back, Kotter" und wird fast über Nacht zum Fernsehstar. Vinnie Barbarino ist ein aggressiver Teenager aus Brooklyn, der die Schule haßt, der gut aussieht und dem die Mädchen nachlaufen.

Was denkt der Lehrer, Herr Kotter?
Stellen Sie einige Fragen an Herrn Travolta-Barbarino!
Sagen Sie etwas über Horshak!

Mit vierundzwanzig spielt er Tony Manero, den Disco-König aus Brooklyn, in *Saturday Night Fever*. John Travolta and Disco werden mit diesem Film weltberühmt.° Die Schallplatte° mit der Musik der Bee Gees schlägt alle Verkaufsrekorde° für Filmmusik.

Mit neunundzwanzig spielt Travolta noch einmal Tony Manero. Weil *Saturday Night Fever* so ein großer Erfolg° war, macht der Filmproduzent Stigwood eine Fortsetzung.° (Das kennen wir nun schon von Hollywood.) Die Fortsetzung heißt *Staying Alive*. In diesem Film geht Tony Manero von Brooklyn über die Brooklyn Bridge nach Manhattan, um am Broadway Karriere zu machen. Der Film zeigt den Aufstieg Tony Maneros vom unbekannten,° unorthodoxen Tänzer zum Broadway-Star. Natürlich gibt es im Film eine Liebesgeschichte,° phantastische Tanzszenen und Musik von den Bee Gees.

John Travolta ist kein Aussteiger,° der gegen Eltern, Schule und Gesellschaft° protestiert. "Ich bin das Produkt eines glücklichen Familienlebens," erklärt er den Reportern seinen Erfolg. John Travoltas Werte sind traditionell, wenn wir den Biographen° und Filmjournalisten glauben dürfen. John Travolta möchte heiraten und viele Kinder haben. Er wartet noch auf die Frau, die ihn liebt und Mutter seiner Kinder werden soll. Für alle Damen, die Frau Travolta werden wollen, haben wir einige wichtige Hinweise:° John Travolta mag Frauen, die unabhängig° sind und ihre eigene Karriere haben. "Ein nettes Wesen° ist wichtiger als ein hübsches° Gesicht," meint John Travolta.

In allen Rollen spielt Travolta ein bißchen sein eigenes Leben und zugleich° den Traum° vieler Amerikaner und Amerikanerinnen. Sie wollen aus der Anonymität einer einfachen Existenz ausbrechen,° berühmt° werden und natürlich viel Geld verdienen. Sie träumen von einer Karriere als Schauspieler,° Tänzer° oder Sänger° am Broadway oder in Hollywood. John Travolta hat es geschafft. Kein Wunder,° daß sich Millionen mit ihm identifizieren. Stars wie Travolta erlauben es Millionen Amerikanern und Amerikanerinnen, den amerikanischen Traum zu träumen:° den Traum von Glück, Reichtum° und Popularität.

worldfamous
record
sales records

success
continuation, sequel

unknown
love story

drop-out
society

biographers

hints
independent
disposition, character
pretty
at the same time
dream
break out
famous
actor
dancer
singer
wonder
dream
wealth

A **PLAY WITH ELEMENTS FROM THE TEXT.** Use these suggestions for exercises to activate your experience and your imagination and your knowledge of German. You will be surprised how much you can already say in German. Comments and questions should be welcome after each statement.

1. Mit sechzehn wollte ich _____.

   darf man _____.

   dürfen die Amerikaner _____.

   habe ich _____.

   _____.

2. In der Schule war es (ist es) _____.

    machen die Schüler _____.

    müssen die Lehrer _____.

    _____.

3. Im Supermarkt sieht man _____.

    gibt es _____.

    können wir _____.

    dürfen wir nicht _____.

    _____.

4. Für 25 Dollar würde ich drei Schallplatten kaufen.

    würde ich _____.

    _____.

5. Schauspieler haben viele Freunde.

    brauchen _____.

    verdienen _____.

6. Teenager sind _____.

    möchten _____.

    fahren _____.

7. Die Bee Gees singen _____.

    haben _____.

    verkaufen _____.

8. Ich möchte nicht in Manhattan wohnen.

    Die Luft _____.

    Es gibt zuviel(e) _____.

    Man kann nicht _____.

9. Ich möchte in Manhattan wohnen.

Manhattan ist _____.

Manhattan hat _____.

Man kann in Manhattan _____.

10. Aussteiger gehen nicht _____.

protestieren gegen _____.

wollen nicht _____.

rauchen _____.

_____.

11. In einer glücklichen Familie arbeiten Vater und Mutter.
    helfen die Kinder beim Aufräumen.

_____

_____

B HOW DO THESE GROUPS OF PEOPLE INTERACT?

die Schüler ⟷ die Lehrer
die Eltern ⟷ die Lehrer
die Schüler ⟷ die Eltern

Use the verbs below for your statements and expect to be questioned.

fragen	was fragen sie, z.B.?	
helfen	wie?	
respektieren	warum?	
geben Hausaufgaben°	was für?	homework
kritisieren	was?	
protestieren gegen	warum? wogegen?	
streiken	warum?	
rebellieren gegen	was tun sie? wogegen?	
lehren° (unterrichten)°	was?	to teach / to teach
zuhören (gut, schlecht, nie)	warum?	
bewundern°	warum?	admire
ärgern°	wie?	to annoy, make angry
brauchen	warum?	
sprechen mit	worüber?	
diskutieren° mit	worüber?	to discuss
fürchten°	warum?	to fear

C FRAGEN, FRAGEN, FRAGEN UND AUFGABEN

*to leave
high school
diploma*

1. Warum verlassen° einige Schüler die Oberschule° ohne Abschluß?°

   _____

   _____

   _____

2. Möchten Sie in New Jersey wohnen? Wenn ja, warum? Wenn nein, warum nicht? (Consider the ocean, the oil industry, chemical industry, proximity to New York, whether you have friends there, etc.)

   _____

   _____

   _____

actor

3. Möchten Sie Schauspieler(in)° werden? Wenn ja, warum? Wenn nein, warum nicht?

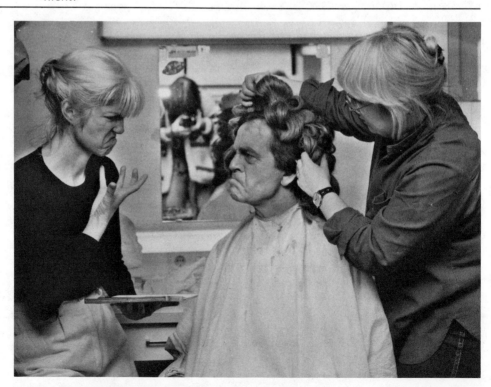

Schauspieler
müssen ...
Schauspieler
möchten ... Wie
leben
Schauspieler?

_____
_____
_____

4. Ich möchte Rechtsanwalt (Rechtsanwältin)° werden, weil _____. *lawyer*

   Arzt (Ärztin) werden, weil _____.

   Pilot(in) werden, weil _____.

   Schriftsteller(in)° werden, weil _____. *writer*

   Kaufmann werden, weil _____.

   Fußballspieler(in) werden, weil _____.

5. Haben Sie schon einmal im Supermarkt gearbeitet? (Those who have not should report on any other activity for which they were paid.)
   a. Was haben Sie gemacht?

   _____

   b. Wie hat Ihnen die Arbeit gefallen? (give reasons)

   _____

   c. Was können Sie über Ihre Arbeitskolleg(inn)en sagen?

   _____

   d. Was können Sie über Ihren Chef sagen?

   _____

   e. Was haben Sie gelernt?
   Ich habe gelernt, daß_____.
   Ich habe _____ gelernt.

6. Was ist Ihr Traum?
   Mein Traum ist, auf Hawaii zu wohnen.

   _____
   _____
   _____

7. Haben Sie schon einmal eine Episode von *Welcome Back, Kotter* gesehen? Wenn ja:

a. Warum gefällt Ihnen diese Fernseh-Serie? Warum nicht?

b. Was für ein Lehrer ist Herr Kotter?

c. Können Sie etwas über Horshak sagen?

d. Erzählen Sie eine Szene oder Episode aus *Welcome Back, Kotter!*

high school   e. Wie war es in Ihrer Oberschule?°

In einer deutschen Schule. Was ist anders als in einer amerikanischen Schule? Was ist gleich? Was würde Herr Travolta-Barbarino zum Lehrer sagen?

_____

f. Was halten° Sie von° Vinnie Barbarino? Ist er Ihnen sympathisch?° Ist er
Ihnen unsympathisch? Warum?

think of
likeable, congenial

_____

10. Wenn Sie *Welcome Back, Kotter* nie gesehen haben, sprechen Sie bitte über
eine andere populäre Fernsehserie, die Sie mögen. Let your classmates elicit
information from you by asking you questions.

_____

_____

_____

_____

11. Sie besitzen° eine Fernsehstation. Machen Sie Ihr Fernsehprogramm, wie Sie es
wünschen. z.B.
Um acht Uhr morgens sende° ich 30 Minuten Nachrichten ohne Reklame.°

own

broadcast
advertisement

Von 9 bis 10 Uhr morgens zeige ich den Film _____.

Um 11 Uhr abends bringe ich ein Interview _____.

Von 12 bis 1 zeige ich, wie ich _____.

_____

_____

12. Haben Sie *Saturday Night Fever* oder *Staying Alive* gesehen? Wenn ja:
a. Was hat Ihnen gefallen? Warum?
b. Was hat Ihnen nicht gefallen? Warum?

Mir hat _____ gefallen.

Mir hat es gefallen, als _____

_____

13. Die Bee Gees kommen aus Australien.
Was wissen Sie über Australien? (consider animals, climate, language, sports,
your interest in the country, clichés, etc.)

_____

_____

_____

14. Halten Sie John Travolta für einen guten Schauspieler? Warum? Warum nicht?

_____

_____

_____

sequels

15. Wir kennen viele Fortsetzungen:° *Rocky I, Rocky II, Rocky III, Superman I, II, III, Jaws I, II, III,* usw. Warum macht Hollywood so viele Fortsetzungen?

_____

_____

16. Was für eine Rolle möchten Sie im Film spielen?

_____

17. Was verlangen traditionelle Werte von uns?
    Wir sollen arbeiten.
    Wir sollen heiraten und Kinder haben.

must not steal, are expected to save money, love our parents, respect the government, shall vote, must dress, may not drink too much, etc.

_____

_____

_____

_____

think of
dream

18. Was halten° Sie vom° amerikanischen Traum?° Warum?

    Ich finde den _____.

    Ich halte den _____.

    _____

advantages
famous

19. Vorteile,° wenn man berühmt° ist.

    Man kann _____.

    Man darf _____.

    Man hat _____.

    Man sieht _____.

disadvantages

20. Nachteile,° wenn man berühmt ist.

    Alle Leute wollen _____.

Man kann nicht _____.

Man muß _____.

21. Warum gehen viele Leute ins Kino?

_____

_____

D WHAT COULD THEY SAY TO EACH OTHER?

1. Travolta—Muhammad Ali
   Travolta: "Ali, ich bin der Schönste!"
   Ali: "Du träumst, John. Ich bin schöner und intelligenter als du!"

   _____

   _____

2. Einstein—Brooke Shields.
   Brooke Shields: "Herr Einstein, tragen Sie auch Jeans?"
   Einstein: "Fräulein Shields, wieviel ist eins und eins?"

   _____

   _____

3. Ronald Reagan—Fidel Castro

   _____

   _____

4. Beethoven—Elvis Presley

   _____

   _____

5. Johnny Carson—Dick Cavett

   _____

   _____

6. Hugh Hefner—Gloria Steinem

   _____

   _____

7. Gott—der Teufel°   *devil*

   _____

_____

_____

8. ein Republikaner—ein Demokrat

_____

_____

_____

Invent your own pair of contrasting public figures and their statements:

_____

_____

ESSENTIAL GRAMMAR: Questions And Question Words:

"General" or "yes-no" questions

Tanzen Sie gern?
Geht Herr Travolta gern aus?
Geht Herr Travolta gern schwimmen?
Ist der Film wirklich so schlecht?
Hast du bei McDonalds gegessen?
Wird der Präsident die Inflation stoppen?

lend Kannst du mir einen Dollar leihen?°

Observe the word order in these questions: conjugated verbs *always* come first, followed by the subject. The conjugated verb can be a full verb (**tanzen**), the main element of a separable expression (**geht**), an auxiliary (**ist, hast, wird**), or a modal (**kannst**).

"Specific" questions

Specific questions begin with an interrogative; the conjugated verb is second, the subject third:

Was hat Johnny Carson über den Film gesagt?

magnetic tape Wessen Tonband° ist das?

Warum möchten Sie nicht in Hollywood leben?

Mit wem haben Sie heute ein Bier getrunken?

Wofür interessieren Sie sich, Herr Travolta?

Wer fährt einen Alfa Romeo?

Note the end position of participles and infinitives (like the word order in statements).

Interrogatives:

Persons	Things
wer? who? (nominative, asking for the subject of a sentence)	**was?** what? (nominative)
wen? whom? (accusative, asking for the direct object of a sentence)	**was?** what? (accusative)
wem? whom? to whom? (dative, asking for the indirect object of a sentence)	
wessen? whose? (genitive or possessive case, asking for the owner)	
für wen? for whom?	**wofür?** for what?
mit wem? with whom?	**womit?** with what?
	Worüber? about what? (an "r" is slipped in between vowels)
preposition followed by appropriate interrogative	**wo** + preposition

was für . . .?

was für ein Mann? what kind of man?
was für eine Frau? what kind of woman?
was für ein Kind? what kind of child?
was für Männer (Frauen, Kinder)? what kind of men, women, children?

was für is followed by the indefinite article and a noun; in the plural there is, of course, no article.

welcher, welche, welches?

welcher Mann? which man?
welche Frau? which woman?
welches Kind? which child?
welche Männer? (Frauen, Kinder)? which men, women, children?

"**welch-**" followed by an appropriate ending and noun in the respective cases.

Asking for place, time, cause, and other aspects

wo? where? (asking for a place or location)

wohin? where, where . . . to? (movement toward a goal, destination)

woher? where . . . from?

wann? when?

warum? why?

wie? how? **wie groß?** how tall? (and many other combinations)

wie lange? how long? (indicating duration)

wieviel? how much?

wie viele? how many?

A Occasionally it is fun to take a list of words, arranged alphabetically or according to some other principle, and use it as a guideline for a story. In this case, the interrogatives were used to write up questions for an interview with Johnny Carson. **ASK THE QUESTIONS IN SEQUENCE** to elicit answers (the person who gives the answer should ask the next question).

1. Wer verdient mehr Geld als Sie, Herr Carson?
2. Was essen Sie am liebsten?
3. Wen werden Sie nächste Woche einladen?°

invite

4. Wem geben Sie Ihre alten Anzüge?
5. Wessen Stimme können Sie imitieren?
6. Für wen arbeiten Sie?
7. Mit wem korrespondieren Sie?
8. Wofür interessieren Sie sich?
9. Womit kann ich Ihnen eine Freude machen?
10. Worüber sprechen Sie mit Ihrer Frau?
11. Was für einen Wagen fahren Sie?
12. Welche Filme gefallen Ihnen besonders?
13. Wo machen Sie nächstes Jahr Ferien?
14. Wohin fliegen Sie morgen?
15. Woher bekommen Sie Ihre Ideen?
16. Wann beginnt Ihre Show?
17. Warum machen Sie keine Filme?
18. Wie finden Sie Burbank?
19. Wie groß sind Sie?
20. Wie lange dauert Ihre Show?

21. Wieviel kostet Ihr Jackett?
22. Wie viele Sprachen sprechen Sie?

B **USE THE SAME SEQUENCE OF INTERROGATIVES** in developing interview questions for a different celebrity. Use different verbs.

KAPITEL 11

zwischen Morgen und Abend

Retracing your activities on any average day is a useful task for a language learner. It produces a wealth of practical vocabulary, and your experiences—shared to varying degrees by your classmates—provide an immediate communicative bond. Everybody has to get up some time during the day and most people go to sleep at the end of the day. The time in between is taken up by activities most people share: having breakfast, going to work, having a lunch break, reading the newspaper or watching TV, going shopping, etc. As your statements are questioned or commented upon by other students, you will find yourself clarifying what you said and providing additional information. Retracing your day should lead to pleasant, productive exchanges about various aspects of everybody's day. Deviations from the norm (no breakfast, no work, not even getting up) will probably be the most challenging contributions.

EIN TAG IN UNSEREM LEBEN

alarm clock rings

1.	Der Wecker° klingelt.°	Wer weckt Sie? Ihre Mutter? Das Radio?
2.	Draußen ist es noch dunkel.	Im Sommer?
3.	Ich mache Licht.	Warum brauchen Sie Licht?
4.	Ich stehe auf.	Steht Ihr Mann (Ihre Frau) auch auf?
5.	Ich gehe ins Badezimmer.	Wie fühlen Sie sich am Morgen?
6.	Ich sehe in den Spiegel.	Was sehen Sie?
7.	Ich sehe noch müde aus.	Warum sehen Sie noch müde aus?
8.	Ich putze mir die Zähne.	Mit einer elektrischen Zahnbürste?
9.	Ich dusche mich.	Duschen Sie sich warm oder kalt?
10.	Ich wasche mir die Haare.	Wie oft waschen Sie sich die Haare?
11.	Ich rasiere mich (nicht).	Warum rasieren sich Männer?
12.	Ich schminke mich (nicht).	Warum schminken sich Frauen?
13.	Ich gehe ins Schlafzimmer zurück.	Wie viele Zimmer hat Ihr Haus (Ihre Wohnung)?
14.	Ich kämme mich (mir die Haare).	Tragen Sie ihr Haar kurz oder lang?
15.	Ich ziehe mich an.	Was tragen Sie am liebsten?

A MAKE SURE YOU UNDERSTAND each sentence in column 1 by reading it in sequence. Ask for the meaning of unknown words or phrases.

B ONE STUDENT READS A SENTENCE from column 1, a second the following question from column 2. The question may elicit as many answers as may be provided by the class with ease.

C ONE HALF OF THE CLASS CUES THE OTHER HALF by reading one or two words from the statements in column 1. Follow the sequence. Do it again with roles reversed.

EXAMPLE:

Der Wecker . . .	Der Wecker klingelt.
. . . noch dunkel	Draußen ist es noch dunkel.

D REPLACE "ICH" IN THE SEQUENCE OF ACTIVITIES by a person not indifferent to the class (maybe Ali, Travolta, Superman, Siegfried, a student with a good sense of humor, etc.). New activities may be added, but retain the original sequence as a guideline. Of course, new questions and answers will have to be provided.

E PUT THE WHOLE SEQUENCE IN THE PRESENT PERFECT or simple past tense.

ACTIVITIES CONTINUED:

16.	Ich gehe in die Küche.	_____?
17.	Ich mache mir Frühstück.	_____?
18.	Ich brate mir zwei Spiegeleier.°	_____? *fried eggs (sunny side up)*
19.	Ich schalte° das Radio an (ein).°	_____? *switch on*
20.	Ich esse zwei Spiegeleier und ein Brötchen° mit Butter und Honig.°	_____? *roll / honey*
21.	Ich trinke eine Tasse Kaffee mit Milch und Zucker.	_____?
22.	Ich höre Nachrichten.	_____?
23.	Ich gehe zur Haustür,° um die Zeitung zu holen.	_____? *front door*
24.	Ich mache die Tür auf.	_____?
25.	Ich nehme die Zeitung.	_____?
26.	Ich mache die Tür wieder zu.	_____?
27.	Ich lese fünf Minuten in der Zeitung.	_____?
28.	Nun ist es höchste Zeit,° zur Arbeit zu fahren.	_____? *high time*
29.	Ich ziehe mir den Mantel an.	_____?
30.	Ich schließe° die Haustür ab.°	_____? *lock*
31.	Ich schließe° meinen Wagen auf.°	_____? *unlock, open*
32.	Ich setze mich ans Steuer.°	_____? *steering wheel*
33.	Ich fahre° los.°	_____? *drive off*
34.	Ich fahre zur Arbeit.	_____?

A MAKE SURE YOU UNDERSTAND each sentence in column 1 by reading it in sequence. Try to guess the meaning of unknown words or ask if necessary.

B ONE STUDENT READS A SENTENCE from column a, the others come up with a question (column 2 can be assigned as homework). These questions should in turn be answered by the first speaker.

C ONE HALF OF THE CLASS CUES THE OTHER HALF by reading one or two words from the statements in column 1. Follow the sequence. Do it again with roles reversed.

EXAMPLE: . . . . . die Küche.   Ich gehe in die Küche.

D TELL US MORE ABOUT YOUR DAY: your activities and experiences on the way to work (to the university, your school), at work, during the lunch break, in the afternoon, on your way home, activities after work. During each stage of daily experience, as many students as possible should contribute.

EXAMPLE: Student 1: Ich fahre immer 60 Meilen pro Stunde.
Student 2: Ich fahre mit meinem Freund. Er fährt immer zu langsam.
Student 3: Ich fahre mit dem Bus. Der Busfahrer fährt wie ein Rennfahrer.

AUF DEM WEG ZUR ARBEIT (ZUR UNIVERSITÄT, ZUR SCHULE)

	schnell fahren
to get angry about	sich über schlechte Autofahrer ärgern°
to honk	hupen°
to get into a traffic jam	in einen Verkehrsstau geraten °
	nervös werden
	sich verspäten (zu spät kommen)
to apologize	sich entschuldigen° (beim Chef, bei der Chefin, beim Professor, bei der Professorin)

BEI DER ARBEIT (AN DER UNIVERSITÄT, IN DER SCHULE)

	Briefe schreiben
	telefonieren (mit wem)
to type	tippen°
library	in der Bibliothek° arbeiten

Probleme lösen°   *solve*
Autos verkaufen
Autos reparieren
Kunden bedienen

IN DER MITTAGSPAUSE° UND AM NACHMITTAG   *lunchbreak*

von 12 bis 1 Mittagspause machen
bei McDonalds essen
sich einen großen Mac bestellen
auf der Straße einen Freund (eine Freundin) treffen
sich mit ihm (mit ihr) verabreden
ins Büro zurückgehen
aus dem Fenster schauen°   *to look*
sich auf die Arbeit konzentrieren
eine Tasse Kaffee trinken
sich auf den Feierabend° freuen   *time after work*

Stellen Sie Fragen:
Wer ...? Was ...?
Wo ...? Wann ...?
Wie viele ...?
Warum ...?
Dramatize the
scene by putting
German sentences
into the mouths of
the people in the
picture.

NACH DER ARBEIT

to go shopping	schnell einkaufen° gehen°
to gas up, buy gas	tanken°
	nach Hause fahren
dinner, supper	Abendbrot° essen
	fernsehen
	mit dem Hund spazieren gehen
	Musik hören
to relax	sich entspannen°
	Tennis spielen (mit wem?)
	ein Glas Bier trinken (wo?)

DER MANN, DER ALS KÄFER AUFWACHT
(Nach einer Episode aus Franz Kafkas ,,Die Verwandlung")

traveling salesman	Von Beruf bin ich Vertreter.° Ich verkaufe Schuhe für die Firma Merkur.
on the road, on the go	Als Vertreter bin ich viel unterwegs.°
is true	Ich muß jeden Morgen früh aufstehen. ,,Morgenstunde hat Gold im Munde," so sagt man. Leider stimmt° das nicht, jedenfalls° nicht
at any rate	für mich.
on the road	Viel verdiene ich nicht, obwohl ich jeden Tag 12 Stunden auf der Achse° bin; und das 6 Tage in der Woche!
most of the time	Meistens° übernachte° ich in billigen Hotels.
stay overnight	
boss	Vor meinem Chef° habe ich Angst. Er ist sehr mißtrauisch.°
distrustful	Am liebsten möchte er, daß ich Tag und Nacht unterwegs bin.
single (not married)	Ich bin ledig° und wohne noch bei meinen Eltern.
6 Uhr 30:	Ich habe schlecht geschlafen.
bad	Ich habe böse° Träume° gehabt.
dreams	
doze	Ich liege auf dem Rücken und döse° noch ein bißchen.
	Was ich jetzt vor mir sehe, ist kein Traum mehr.
	Mein Bauch ist braun und hart wie die Unterseite eines Insekts.
	Vor meinen Augen bewegen sich viele kleine dünne Beine.
	Ich kann sie nicht zählen.
beetle, bug	Ich weiß es jetzt ganz bestimmt: über Nacht bin ich ein Käfer° geworden.

6 Uhr 45:   Ich muß unbedingt° zur Arbeit. Ich muß mich beeilen.°   *definitely, absolutely*
             Was wird mein Chef sagen, wenn ich zu spät komme?   *hurry*

             Sicher wird er schimpfen.° Vielleicht wird er mich entlassen.°   *scold*
             Aber wie komme ich aus dem Bett?   *dismiss, fire*

6 Uhr 50:   Meine Mutter hat gerade an die Tür geklopft.° Sie hat gesagt: *knocked*
             "Junge, du mußt aufstehen. Dein Zug fährt in 20 Minuten."

             Ich habe ihr geantwortet: "Gleich, Mutter. Ich bin gleich fertig."

             Mein Vater hat gefragt: "Was ist los,° Gregor?"   *What's going on?*

             Ich habe geantwortet: "Nichts ist los. Alles ist in Ordnung."

             Aber mein Vater wollte mir nicht glauben. Er sagte: "Das ist nicht
             Gregors Stimme!"

             Zum Glück konnte niemand in mein Zimmer kommen. Ich
             schließe° jeden Abend die Tür ab.°   *lock*

7 Uhr: Jetzt höre ich die Stimme meines Chefs.

             Warum mußte denn ausgerechnet° der Chef kommen?   *of all people*

             Warum hat man nicht einen Angestellten° geschickt?   *employee*

             Was soll meine Familie denken, wenn man mich wie einen
             Verbrecher° sucht?   *criminal, gangster*

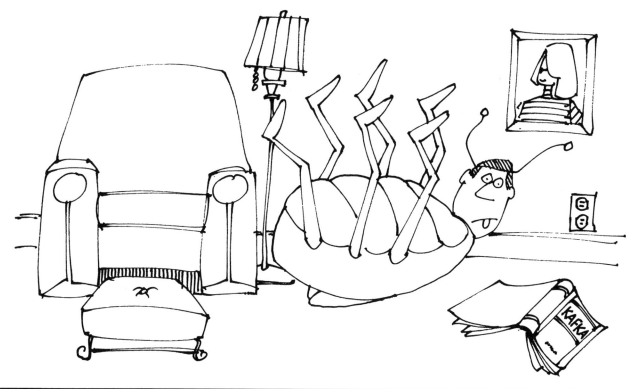

	Der Chef sagte: "Was ist los mit Ihnen, Herr Samsa?
	Fühlen Sie sich nicht wohl?
hide	Warum verstecken° Sie sich?
grief (sorrows)	Sie machen Ihren Eltern große Sorgen.°
be ashamed	Sie sollten sich schämen!°
on the road, on the go	Sie sollten schon längst unterwegs° sein."
got angry	7 Uhr 10: Ich habe mich über die Worte des Chefs sehr geärgert.°
am late	Ich verspäte° mich nie.
	Ich stehe früher auf als meine Kollegen.
time-tables, schedules	Ich kenne die Fahrpläne° der Züge auswendig.
	Ich interessiere mich fast nur für meinen Beruf.
	7 Uhr 12: Ich bin aufgestanden. Sie wollen wissen wie?
rocked back and forth	Ich bin so lange auf dem Rücken hin- und hergeschaukelt,° bis ich aus dem Bett gefallen bin.
	Dabei habe ich mich verletzt.
open	Dann habe ich versucht, die Tür zu öffnen.°

Das ist nicht einfach, wenn man ein Käfer° ist. *bug, beetle*
Ich habe mich dabei verletzt.
Endlich hat sich die Tür geöffnet.
Mein Chef hat vor Schreck nur den Mund aufgerissen.° *gaped*
Er konnte kein Wort sagen.
"Oh," hat er gesagt. Das war alles.
Meine Mutter ist ohnmächtig° geworden. *fainted*
Mein Vater ist wütend° geworden. *furious*
Erst wollte er mich schlagen.
Wer möchte schon einen Käfer als Sohn haben!?
Dann hat er aber nur geweint.
Ich wollte mit dem Chef sprechen.
Ich wollte ihm alles erklären.
Aber der Chef rannte° vor Angst weg. *ran*
Er wäre beinahe° die Treppe hinuntergefallen.° *almost* / *fallen down*
Meine Mutter hat geschrien.
Als mein Vater das sah und hörte, ist er noch wütender geworden.
Er nahm einen Stock und eine Zeitung und versuchte, mich wie ein Tier in mein Zimmer zurückzujagen.
Dabei habe ich mich wieder verletzt.
Dann habe ich vor Wut,° Schmerz° und Enttäuschung° bis zum Abend in meinem Zimmer geschlafen. *rage* / *pain* / *disappointment*

A **WAS IST TYPISCH FÜR EINEN VERTRETER?** Think of travel, almost every night in a different town, staying in hotels, need to always be friendly, dress well, shave well, loneliness, potential marital problems, etc.

_____

_____

_____

B **VERTRETER SIND VIEL UNTERWEGS. WER NOCH UND WARUM?**
(Piloten, Stewardessen, Busfahrer, Taxifahrer, Fußballspieler, Politiker, usw.)
Was ist typisch für ihre Arbeit?

_____

_____

_____

C FRÜHAUFSTEHEN HAT SEINE PROBLEME.

Ich kann _____ nicht finden.

Ich _____
(noch müde, kalt, zu lange schlafen, keine Lust zur Arbeit, Frühstück, usw.)

D "Morgenstunde hat Gold im Munde." ERKLÄREN SIE DAS SPRICHWORT!°

proverb

Wenn man früh aufsteht, .
Wenn man früh aufsteht, .
Stimmt das Sprichwort? Wenn nein, warum nicht?

E VIEL ARBEITEN, WENIG VERDIENEN. How does this affect somebody's life? Think of family, vacations, going to restaurants and bars, concerts, plays, frame of mind of the person affected, etc.

_____

_____

_____

F MEINE WOCHE. Plans for the coming or highlights of the past week.

Am Montag werde ich (habe ich) .
Am Dienstag werde ich (habe ich) .
Am Mittwoch will ich (bin ich) .

G **BILLIGE HOTELS** Discuss experiences, fears, possible advantages.

> Das Zimmer
> Das Essen
> Die Bedienung

H **BEI DEN ELTERN WOHNEN:** Vorteile° und Nachteile.° You may want to use these leads.

advantages
disadvantages

Ich wohne gern bei meinen Eltern, weil _____.

Es ist nicht gut, bei den Eltern zu wohnen, weil _____.

Wenn man bei seinen Eltern wohnt, _____.

I **LEDIG° ODER VERHEIRATET:°** Wer hat mehr vom Leben?

single (not married)
married

> Wenn man ledig ist,
>
> Wenn man verheiratet ist,

J **WAS WÜRDEN SIE TUN,** wenn Sie als Käfer aufwachen?

_____

_____

_____

react

K **WIE REAGIEREN° SIE,** wenn Sie

zu spät zur Arbeit kommen?

_____

zu spät ins Konzert kommen?

_____

appointment, date

zu spät zu einer Verabredung° kommen?

_____

L **IHR VERHÄLTNIS ZU IHRER MUTTER.** Was tut Ihre Mutter für Sie? Was tun Sie für Ihre Mutter? Was tun Sie zusammen? Was kritisiert Ihre Mutter an Ihnen?

M **IHR VERHÄLTNIS ZU IHREM VATER.** Was tut Ihr Vater für Sie? Was tun Sie für Ihren Vater? Was tun Sie zusammen? Was kritisiert Ihr Vater an Ihnen?

N A BAD SITUATION THAT COULD HAVE BEEN WORSE. Think both of personal experience and the world at large.

      EXAMPLES: Ich habe meine Autoschlüssel verloren. Zum Glück habe ich noch einen Schlüssel zu Hause.

              Die Russen und die Amerikaner haben Raketen.° Zum Glück wollen beide keinen Krieg.   *rockets*

O Although Gregor does not react to the questions and reprimands of his boss, YOU CAN ANSWER FOR GREGOR. Be abrasive, timid, conciliatory, be whatever you like.

      EXAMPLE: Herr Samsa, warum sind Sie noch im Bett?

              Ich habe keine Lust,° aufzustehen.   *have no inclination, do not feel like*

P WIE WÜRDEN IHRE VERWANDTEN UND FREUNDE REAGIEREN, wenn Sie als Käfer aus dem Zimmer kämen?°   *came (subjunctive)*

Q Gregor Samsa hat sich verletzt, als er aus dem Bett gefallen ist. WOBEI HABEN SIE SICH SCHON EINMAL VERLETZT? Was war das Resultat?

EXAMPLE: Ich habe mich beim Skilaufen verletzt. Ich habe mir den Arm gebrochen.

_____

_____

_____

_____

 Tünnes and Schäl are the "heroes" of innumerable jokes told in the area around Cologne and in the Rhineland in general. They reflect the spirit of a wine-drinking, fun-loving people. But Tünnes and Schäl are also good Catholics and democrats.

Pope

TÜNNES: Hast du gehört, Schäl, daß der Papst° tot ist?

SCHÄL: Ja, das ist sehr traurig.

elect

TÜNNES: Aber in Rom wählen° sie wieder einen neuen Papst.

election

SCHÄL: Ja, aber das ist doch keine richtige Wahl.°

TÜNNES: Aber warum nicht, Schäl?

SCHÄL: Die nehmen doch wieder einen Katholiken!

ESSENTIAL GRAMMAR: Reflexive Verbs and Pronouns

Klaus wäscht das Auto.
("normal," non-reflexive object)

Klaus wäscht sich.
(reflexive pronoun as object)

Reflexive pronouns are used when the subject of a sentence is also the object of its action. The reflexive pronoun can function as a direct object, or, in the presence of another direct object, as an indirect object. (This is most frequent when referring to parts of your body.)

COMPARE: **Ich wasche mich.**
Ich wasche mir die Hände.

Both English and German have reflexive verbs. Unfortunately, most German reflexive verbs are not reflexive in English. Fortunately, you only have to learn one additional form, namely **sich** for the third-person singular and plural and the formal **Sie.**

For the rest, the accusative and dative of the personal pronoun also function as reflexive pronouns (see the chart). Another observation: the accusative and dative forms of the reflexive pronoun are identical except for the **ich-** and **du-** forms (see the chart).

PERSONAL PRONOUN			REFLEXIVE PRONOUN	
Nominative	Accusative	Dative	Accusative	Dative
ich	mich	mir	mich	mir
du	dich	dir	dich	dir
er	ihn	ihm		
sie	sie	ihr	sich	
es	es	ihm		
wir	uns		uns	
ihr	euch		euch	
sie	sie	ihnen	sich	
Sie	Sie	Ihnen		

KAPITEL 12

FRAGEN
FRAGEN
FRAGEN...

We grow up with questionnaires. Various authorities and institutions want to know how old we are, where we live, whether we are male or female, single or married, the number of our dependents, etc., etc. Most of us find this intrusion into our private lives quite obnoxious.

In the context of a foreign language class the questionnaire can be stimulating and entertaining. The juxtaposition of fairly serious and quite trivial questions in the subsequent **Fragebogen** and **Die Welt in Ottos Kopf** is intended to set a light, parodistic tone. They should generate many answers and encourage even more questions.

questionnaire

FRAGEBOGEN°

1. Sind Sie glücklich?

   Ich bin glücklich, weil _____.

   Ich bin unglücklich, weil _____.

2. Warum wohnen Sie in den USA? _____
   Welche Nachteile° hat es, in den USA zu wohnen?

   _____

   In welchem anderen Land möchten Sie leben? Warum?

   _____

3. Wie alt möchten Sie werden? _____

   Warum ist es schön, sehr alt zu werden? _____
   Warum ist es nicht so schön, sehr alt zu werden?

   _____

prejudice

4. Haben Sie Vorurteile?°

   Gegen wen haben Sie Vorurteile? _____

   Wogegen haben Sie Vorurteile? _____

5. Interessieren Sie sich für Politik? Wenn ja:
   Für welchen Politiker interessieren Sie sich? Warum?

   _____

domestic policy
foreign policy
trade unions
armament policy

   Wofür interessieren Sie sich in der Politik?
   (zum Beispiel: **e** Innenpolitik,° **e** Außenpolitik,° **e** Gewerkschaften° (*pl*),
   Rüstungspolitik,° Finanzpolitik).

   _____

6. Welche Zahnpasta benutzen Sie? Warum?

   _____

grades
unemployment

7. Wovor fürchten Sie sich? (zum Beispiel: **r** Atomkrieg, **e** Prüfung, **s** Altwerden,
   schlechte Zensuren,° **e** Arbeitslosigkeit°)

   _____

8. Worüber freuen Sie sich am meisten?

   _____

   Ich freue mich am meisten über _____.

   Ich freue mich am meisten, wenn _____.

Ich freue mich am meisten darüber, daß ————————————.

9. Warum möchten Sie heiraten?

   ————————————————————————

   Warum möchten Sie nicht heiraten?

   ————————————————————————

   Warum gibt es heute so viele Ehescheidungen°   *divorces*

   ————————————————————————

10. Was halten Sie von der Königin° von England?   *queen*

    Ich finde die Königin von England ————————————.

    Ich finde, daß ————————————————.

11. Woran denken Sie, wenn Sie das Wort ''Ferien'' hören?

    Ich denke an ————————————————.

    Ich denke daran, daß ————————————.

12. Wie oft gehen Sie pro Jahr zum Zahnarzt? (einmal, zweimal, dreimal, . . .?)

    _____

13. Was für Wein trinken Sie gern? (Rotwein, Weißwein, kalifornischer Wein, Rheinwein, Moselwein, . . .)

    _____

14. Sind Sie optimistisch? Warum? _____

    Sind Sie pessimistisch? Warum? _____

15. Wie würde Ihr Leben ohne Auto aussehen?

    _____

16. Bleiben Sie gern lange auf? Wenn ja:
    Was machen Sie zwischen 10 und 12 Uhr abends?

    _____

stay up   17. Warum bleiben° Sie nicht gern lange auf?°

    _____

18. Warum stehen Sie gern früh auf? Warum stehen Sie ungern früh auf?

    _____

19. Wie lange wohnen Sie schon in dieser Stadt?

    _____

    Wie gefällt Ihnen die Stadt? Warum?

    _____

20. Haben Sie Humor? Warum glauben Sie das?

    _____

sick with a cold   21. Was machen Sie, wenn Sie erkältet° sind und Fieber° haben?
fever

    _____

22. Wer näht den Knopf an, wenn ein Knopf an Ihrem Mantel, Ihrer Hose oder Ihrer

    Jacke fehlt?_____

23. Was erwarten Sie von einem guten Lehrer?

    Ein guter Lehrer soll (muß, darf nicht)_____

past   24. Denken Sie einmal an Ihre Vergangenheit!°
experience   Was war bisher° Ihr schönstes Erlebnis° (Ihr größter Erfolg)?°
success
up to now

    _____

    Mein schönstes Erlebnis war, als _____.
    Was war bisher Ihr traurigstes Erlebnis?

    _____

25. Was würden Sie mit einer Million Dollar machen?

    _____

26. Haben Sie als Kind (oder Teenager) einmal einen Erwachsenen° geärgert?   *adult*

    Was haben Sie gemacht? _____

27. Worüber ärgern Sie sich am meisten oder besonders?

    Ich ärgere mich am meisten über _____.

    Ich ärgere mich immer, wenn _____.

    Ich ärgere mich besonders darüber, daß _____.

28. Waren Sie schon einmal in einem deutschen Dorf? Wie sieht es da aus?
    (Wenn Sie keine Erfahrung haben, denken Sie an Max und Moritz)

    _____

Haben Sie schon einmal protestiert? Wann? Wo? Wogegen? Wie haben die Polizisten (die Leute auf der Straße) reagiert?

29. Haben Sie schon einmal protestiert? Wenn ja:
Wogegen haben Sie protestiert? oder: Gegen wen haben Sie protestiert?

Warum? _____

nuclear armament Warum protestieren Sie nicht gegen die Atomaufrüstung?°

_____

discuss 30. Worüber diskutieren° Sie häufig° in Ihrer Familie?
frequently

_____

31. Was tragen Sie am liebsten? Warum?

_____

32. Wann photographieren Sie meistens? Warum? _____

Was photographieren Sie meistens? _____

33. Wo wollen Sie später einmal wohnen? Warum dort?

_____

34. Was erwarten° Sie von Ihrem Haus oder Ihrer Wohnung?   *expect*

    Es muß (soll) _____ .

35. Hören Sie gern Witze?° Warum? Warum nicht?   *jokes*

    _____

36. Erzählen Sie gern Witze? Warum? Warum nicht?

    _____

Warum lachen die beiden Männer und die Frau? Was hat der Mann in der Mitte vielleicht gesagt? Was hat die Frau vielleicht gesagt?

37. Wie reagieren° Sie, wenn Sie fliegen?   *react*

    _____

38. Was bedeutet° Armut° für Sie?   *means*
    poverty

    Armut bedeutet für mich, wenn _____ .

39. Was tun Sie, wenn Sie nervös° sind?   *nervous*

    _____

40. Möchten Sie Präsident (Präsidentin) der Vereinigten Staaten werden? Warum? Warum nicht?

    _____

41. Was für Menschen haben Sie besonders gern?

    Ich mag Menschen, die _____ .

42. Add your own questions that you would like to ask of your classmates.

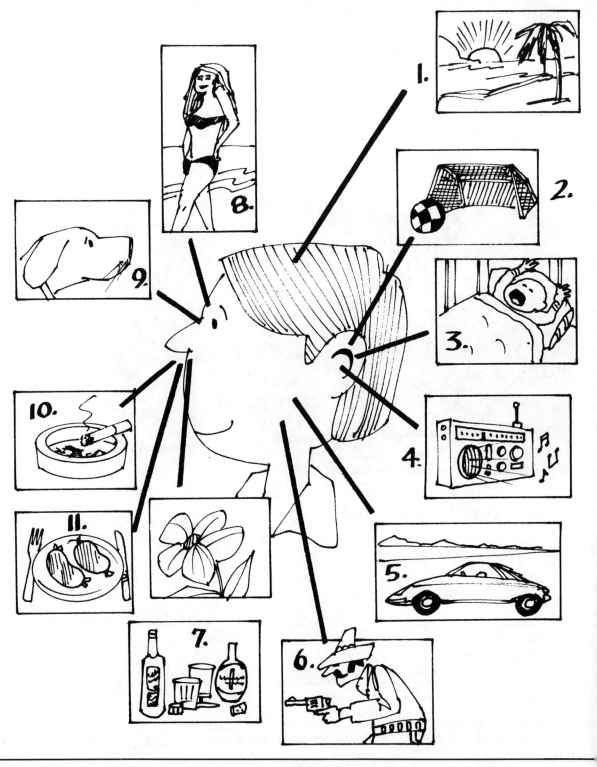

DIE WELT IN OTTOS KOPF

The **Fragebogen** with its mixture of trivial and important, objective and subjective items was intended to bring out some of the innumerable thoughts, opinions, feelings and prejudices present in everybody's mind that can be tapped through questioning. The pictures surrounding Otto's head show just a few of the thousands of associations passing through Otto's mind. Explore the pictures as starting points for conjectures, guesses, and speculations. Also establish relationships between several associations illustrated in the pictures. You may project Otto's perceptions and thoughts into the present, past, or future.

BILD 1: WORAN DENKT OTTO?

_____

Warum möchte er dort sein?

_____

Wird es ihm dort gefallen? Warum? Warum nicht?

_____

Was soll er mitnehmen?

_____

Come up with more questions and comments concerning Otto in relation to picture 1.

BILD 2: OTTO—EIN FUSSBALL—EIN TOR. Speculate about Otto in relation to the game of soccer.

Möchte Otto _____?

    ANSWER: _____

Hat Otto als Junge _____?

    ANSWER: _____

Other questions and comments:

_____

_____

married

BILD 3: OTTO UND DAS BABY. Speculate: Ottos Baby? Otto als Baby? Ottos Bruder oder Schwester? Otto — Babysitter? Otto — verheiratet?° Ottos Frau — wo? Wer? Warum nicht hier?

_____

_____

_____

beach
portable radio

BILD 4: OTTO UND SEIN KOFFERRADIO. Some cues: zu Hause, bei der Arbeit, beim Picknick, am Strand.° Hat Otto ein Kofferradio?° Was hört er gern? Otto — sein Kofferradio — seine Frau (Freundin), Otto — sein Kofferradio — die Familie von nebenan

_____

_____

_____

racing car
car race

BILD 5: OTTO UND DAS AUTO. Ein Mercedes? Ein VW? Ein Rennwagen?° Auf dem Weg zur Arbeit, in die Ferien, beim Autorennen° von Indianapolis, Otto — das Auto—die Polizei, Otto — das Auto — seine Frau (seine Freundin), Otto — das Auto — sein Hund

_____

_____

_____

BILD 6: WER IST DER MANN AUF DEM BILD? Otto selbst? Sein Vater? Sein Onkel in Amerika? John Wayne? Otto als Cowboy in Amerika?

_____

_____

_____

BILD 7: OTTO UND DER ALKOHOL. Hat Otto getrunken? Wenn ja: wann, wo, wieviel? Mit wem? Warum?

_____

_____

_____

Warum trinkt Otto jetzt nicht mehr? (possible reasons: an accident, headaches, wife does not like it, now prefers milk, etc.)

_____

_____

_____

BILD 8: WER IST DIE JUNGE DAME? You may entertain the wildest speculations.

_____

Warum denkt Otto an die junge Dame?

_____

Was hat die junge Dame mit Bild 1 zu tun?

_____

Warum denkt Otto an die junge Dame und das Auto?

_____

Stellen Sie eine Beziehung° zwischen Otto, der jungen Dame auf Bild 8 und dem Cowboy auf Bild 6 her.

relationship

_____

_____

_____

Versuchen Sie, andere Beziehungen° zwischen Otto, der Dame auf Bild 8 und anderen Bildern herzustellen.°

establish relationships

_____

_____

_____

BILD 9: OTTO — DER HUND.

Wessen Hund? _____
Wo sieht Otto den Hund? (draußen vor dem Haus? im Fernsehen? im Kino? bei Freunden? im Büro?)

_____

_____

Was erwartet der Hund von Otto?

Er erwartet, daß Otto _____.

       daß _____.

Was möchte Otto dem Hund sagen?

Du mußt _____.

Hast du _____?

Du darfst nicht _____.

Stellen Sie eine Beziehung zwischen dem Hund und Bild 10 her.

_____

_____

_____

BILD 10: OTTO RIECHT DEN RAUCH VON EINER ZIGARETTE.

Raucht Otto? Wenn ja, warum?_____

Wenn nein, wer raucht? _____

Wo? _____

Wie reagiert Otto? _____

invent Raucher und Nichtraucher. Erfinden° Sie Argumente für beide Gruppen:

Raucher	**Nichtraucher**
_____	_____
_____	_____
_____	_____
_____	_____

Jokes about life in the *DDR* (Deutsche Demokratische Republik, often referred to as East Germany) still center around things people cannot do or say because it is against the official party line. Here is an example.

Zwei Volkspolizisten° stehen an der Mauer in Ostberlin.

people's policemen (police in the German Democratic Republic)
think of
I'm sorry
arrest

Der eine heißt Karl, der andere heißt Otto.
Otto sagt zu Karl: "Du, Karl, was hältst° du von° unserer Regierung?"
Da sagt Karl: "Das Gleiche, was du von unserer Regierung hältst."
Da sagt Otto: "Tut mir leid,° Karl, dann muß ich dich verhaften."°

ESSENTIAL GRAMMAR: Wo- And *Da*-Compounds

Things and Concepts	**Persons Only**

Wogegen protestieren Sie?
    Ich protestiere **gegen die Atomraketen**.
    Die Kirche hat auch **dagegen** protestiert.
Woran denkst Du?
    Ich denke **an die Deutschprüfung**.
    Komisch, **daran** habe ich auch gedacht.

Gegen wen spielen Sie?
    Ich spiele **gegen Herrn McEnroe**.

    Ich habe noch nie **gegen ihn** gespielt.
Bei wem wohnen Sie?
    Ich wohne **bei Frau Schumacher**.

    Ich wohne schon drei Jahre **bei ihr**.

Wo + preposition is used in questions when referring to things and concepts. To facilitate pronunciation, an **r** is inserted if the preposition begins with a vowel:

In questions, a preposition plus interrogative is used when referring to persons.

wo + über = worüber

wo + an = woran

da + preposition is used in declarative sentences in reference to a prepositional object (for instance: **gegen die Atomraketen°** — **dagegen**). To facilitate pronunciation, an **r** is inserted if the preposition begins with a vowel:

In declarative sentences, a preposition plus personal pronoun is used if the prepositional object is a person: **gegen Herrn McEnroe** — **gegen ihn**).

nuclear rockets

da + auf = darauf

da + unter = darunter

Substituting a brief **da**-compound for a prepositional object avoids lengthy repetition and is a welcome space- and time-saver. It is frequently used and characteristic of spoken as well as written German.

    NOTE: **Never** use **da**- or **wo**-compounds in reference to persons.

KAPITEL 13

"DER APFEL FÄLLT NICHT WEIT VOM STAMM"—

Sprichwörter und Redewendungen

Proverbs and idioms tell you something about the way another people experiences reality. They are usually very vivid and therefore easy to remember. They provide good punchlines for conversations and stories, and, in general, spice up ordinary speech. The purpose of this chapter is to introduce you to some popular German proverbs by "working" with them.

"WIR SITZEN ALLE IN EINEM BOOT"

A **FORM AN ASSOCIATIVE CHAIN** beginning with "das Boot":

_____

_____

_____

B Haben Sie schon einmal mit anderen Leuten in einem kleinen Boot gesessen? **WENN JA, WIE WAR DAS?**

_____

_____

_____

_____

WENN NEIN, WAS KANN PASSIEREN, wenn mehrere Leute in einem kleinen Boot sitzen? (think of problems, too much weight, people starting to fight, people getting scared, danger of capsizing, etc.)

_____
_____
_____

C **WAS WÜRDEN SIE MACHEN,** wenn das Boot kenterte (kentern würde)?

Wenn das Boot aus Holz wäre

_____.
I would hold on to the boat.

Wenn das Boot Schwimmwesten hätte,

_____.
I would take a lifevest.

Wenn das Ufer nicht weit entfernt wäre,

_____.
I would call for help.

_____,

_____.
I would swim ashore.

_____,

_____.
I would wait for help.

_____,

_____.
I would not get nervous.

Wenn Kinder im Boot wären,
Wenn das Boot mitten im Atlantik kenterte,

_____.

_____.
I would pray.

_____,

_____.
I would give up hope.

_____,

D Since this idiom exists in English in almost the same form, and its meaning is obvious, **TRY TO PARAPHRASE** it in German. Here are some cues: we need one another; if the boat sinks, we will all sink; we should help one another; we all want to live; we all want to survive; there is only one boat, and the boat belongs to all, etc.

_____
_____
_____

lies

"LÜGEN° HABEN KURZE BEINE"

A LANGE BEINE, KURZE BEINE

Kurze Beine   .
Mit kurzen Beinen   .
Mit langen Beinen   .
Mir werden die Beine müde, wenn ich   .
Beim Skilaufen kann man sich die Beine brechen.
Beim   die Beine brechen.

B SIE HABEN SICH EIN BEIN GEBROCHEN. Ihr Bein ist in Gips. Think of all the things you would like to do but can't, things that you don't like to do and now don't have to, and other pleasures and discomforts that come with a broken leg in a plaster cast.

C HABEN SIE SCHON EINMAL GELOGEN? Wenn ja:

Wann war das? Das war, als _____

Warum haben Sie gelogen? _____

_____

Hat jemand die Lüge gemerkt? Wenn ja, wie hat diese Person reagiert? _____

_____

Würden Sie wieder lügen? In welcher Situation?

Ich würde wieder lügen, wenn _____ .

_____

D DEVELOP A "CHAIN REACTION" SEQUENCE ABOUT LYING.

Wenn du lügst, hast du ein schlechtes Gewissen°.   *conscience*

Wenn du ein schlechtes Gewissen hast, bist du nervös.°   *nervous*

Wenn du nervös bist,   _____ .

                your parents (will) notice it.

_____ _____ .

                they (will) ask questions.

_____ , _____ .

                you (will) have to answer.

_____ , _____ .

                you (will) tell the truth.

_____ ,

_____ ,

*means
(does…mean)
proverb*

E **WAS BEDEUTET° DAS SPRICHWORT°** "Lügen haben kurze Beine"?

F **ILLUSTRATE THE ASSUMED TRUTH** of the proverb through a little story based on the model provided. Keep it simple.

Günther hat in Mathematik eine Fünf geschrieben. (Eine Fünf in Deutschland ist ein *F* in Amerika.) Er kommt nach Hause und sagt nichts. Sein Vater fragt ihn: "Habt ihr die Mathearbeit schon zurückbekomen?" Günther sagt: "Nein, unser Lehrer hat sie noch nicht nachgesehen."°

checked, corrected

Am nächsten Tag kommt Günthers Klassenkamerad° Thomas zum Spielen. Er hat einen neuen Fußball. "Oh, Thomas," sagt Günthers Vater, "das ist ja ein toller° Fußball! Hast du den zum Geburtstag bekommen?" Günther versucht verzweifelt,° Thomas ein Zeichen zu geben. Aber Thomas sieht das Zeichen nicht. "Nein," sagt Thomas stolz, "wir haben gestern unsere Mathearbeit zurückbekommen, und ich habe eine Eins geschrieben. (Eine Eins ist die beste Note in Deutschland.) Als Belohnung° hat mir mein Vater den Fußball gekauft." Und die Moral von der Geschichte?

classmate

great, phantastic

desperately

reward

"DER APFEL FÄLLT NICHT WEIT VOM STAMM."

A **BRAINSTORM ABOUT "APFEL":** words connected with "Apfel," your likes, dislikes, what "Äpfel" can be used for, stories in which an "Apfel" plays an important part, etc.

B **SIND SIE WIE IHR VATER?** Wenn ja, wie ist Ihr Vater?

EXAMPLE: Mein Vater ist sportlich. Er spielt gern Tennis. Er _____

C **SIND SIE WIE IHRE MUTTER?** Wenn ja, wie ist Ihre Mutter?

EXAMPLE: Meine Mutter interessiert sich für Literatur. Sie liest _____

D Wenn Sie nicht wie Ihr Vater oder Ihre Mutter sind, **WIE SIND SIE?**

EXAMPLE: Ich bin ein ruhiger Typ, nicht sehr sportlich. Ich habe ein Aquarium.

Ich

equivalent

E Wie heißt das entsprechende° englische Sprichwort?

_____

describe

F Wann würden Sie das Sprichwort gebrauchen? **BESCHREIBEN° SIE EINE SITUATION,** auf die das Sprichwort zutrifft!°

"HUNDE, DIE BELLEN, BEISSEN NICHT."

A Haben Sie einen Hund? Wenn ja, beschreiben Sie ihn und **ERZÄHLEN SIE UNS ETWAS VON IHREM HUND.**

B Wenn Sie keinen Hund haben: **WARUM HABEN SIE KEINEN HUND?**

C **WARUM BELLEN HUNDE?**

D **WAS TÄTEN SIE** (würden Sie tun), wenn ein bellender Hund Ihnen folgte?

EXAMPLE: Ich nähme einen Stock (würde einen Stock nehmen).

E **WARUM BEISSEN BELLENDE HUNDE NICHT?**

F **GEBEN SIE BEISPIELE** von Leuten, die "bellen, aber nicht beißen."

"MORGENSTUNDE HAT GOLD IM MUNDE."

A **STEHEN SIE GERN FRÜH AUF?** Wenn ja, warum? Wenn nein, warum nicht?

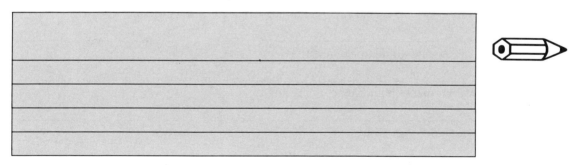

B **DESCRIBE ONE OF YOUR TYPICAL MORNINGS.** Use some of the following cues: The alarm rings; you sleep for another five minutes (or get up immediately), look out of the window to check the weather, walk into the bathroom, take a shower, brush your teeth, wash your hair, comb, get dressed, make coffee or tea, make breakfast, turn on the radio, go the the front door, open the door, pick up the newspaper, close the front door, etc. At any time you may decide to go back to bed.

C Exchange ideas on the following "golden" items as long as ideas and words last:

die Inkakultur   Fort Knox

Gold   die Goldmedaille bei den Olympischen Spielen

der Goldfisch   gold rush

Geld

blessing
curse

D Gold — ein Segen°? Gold — ein Fluch°?

_____

_____

_____

E **WEITERE FRAGEN UND AUFGABEN.**

Warum ist Gold so teuer?

_____

Warum ist unser Geld nicht mehr aus Gold?

_____

wedding
(anniversary)

Was ist eine goldene Hochzeit?°

_____

Warum macht man Zähne aus Gold?

_____

Wie findet man Gold?

_____

Was wissen Sie über die Golden Gate Bridge?

_____

Erklären Sie, was ein Goldhamster ist.

_____

Stellen Sie sich vor: Ihr Auto ist aus Gold. Was würden Sie tun? Was kann passieren?

"WENN DAS WÖRTLEIN WENN NICHT WÄR', WÄR' MEIN VATER MILLIONÄR."

A What if — the curse of missed opportunities, the blessing of avoided catastrophes. **SPECULATE** about what would or would not have happened if . . .

Wenn er den VW nicht gekauft hätte , hätte _____.
*the police would not have stopped
him.*

_____.
he would not have had the accident.

_____.

Wenn Otto geheiratet hätte , _____.
*he would have made his mother
happy.*

_____.

_____.

_____ wäre ich Präsident der Vereinigten
If I had had more money , Staaten geworden.

If I had given more speeches _____ ,

If my friends had helped me _____ ,

If I had been more active _____ ,

If I had gone to bed earlier _____ , wäre ich heute nicht so müde.

If I had not watched the movie _____ ,

If my friends had not stayed so long _____ ,

Wenn du Licht gemacht hättest , _____ .

you would not have fallen.

, _____ .

you would have found your ring.

, _____ .

You would not have broken the glass.

, _____ .

If you had not read the newspaper _____ , _you would not have missed the bus._

If my friend had driven faster _____ , _we would not have been late._

_____ , _____ .

_____ , _____ .

_____ , _____ .

B What could or could not have been. **BEFORE YOU COMPLETE THE FOL-LOWING CUES** you may want to review chapter 2 to 12 in this book.

Wenn Gregor nicht die Tür
aufgemacht hätte , _____ .

Wenn John Travolta nicht Disco
getanzt hätte , _____ .

_____ , wäre Isidor zu Hause geblieben.

_____ , wäre Isidor nicht in die
Fremdenlegion° gekommen.   _foreign legion_

Wenn Muhammad Ali nicht so gut
geboxt hätte   , _____.

Wenn Supermann als Baby auf dem
Planeten Krypton geblieben wäre   , _____.

Wenn Eulenspiegel nicht zwei
Stunden im Gasthaus gesessen hätte   , _____.

_____ , wäre Huckebein nicht gestorben.

_____ , wäre Herr Böck nicht in den Fluß
gefallen.

ESSENTIAL GRAMMAR: The Subjunctive in Wishful Thinking

For oral communication, the most essential aspect of the German subjunctive is
wishful thinking (so-called hypothetical or contrary-to-fact statements). Wishful
thinking will be considered in the two time frames, in which the subjunctive func-
tions, the present/future time frame, and the past time frame.

PRESENT/FUTURE TIME FRAME

1. **Wenn ich Geld hätte,**　　　　　　　**machte ich eine Reise.**
　　　　　　　　　　　　　　　　　　　würde ich eine Reise machen.

　　　(Aber ich habe kein Geld.)
　　If I had money,　　　　　　　　　I would go on a trip.
　　　　(But I don't have the
　　money.)

2. **Wenn Erika käme,**　　　　　　　　**tränke ich ein Glas Wein mit ihr.**
　　　　　　　　　　　　　　　　　　　würde ich ein Glas Wein mit ihr
　　　　　　　　　　　　　　　　　　　trinken.

　　　(Aber sie kommt nicht,)
　　If Erika came,　　　　　　　　　　I would drink a glass of wine with
　　　　　　　　　　　　　　　　　　her.

　　　(But she isn't coming.)

double

3. **Wenn du das Auto von
   diesem Mann kauftest,**   **kostete es doppelt° soviel.**
                                                würde es doppelt soviel kosten.

   (Aber du kaufst es nicht).
   If you bought the
   car from this man,   it would cost twice as much.
                (But you are not buying it.)

FORMS OF THE SUBJUNCTIVE

The subjunctive expressing wishful thinking in the present/future time frame is derived from the past tense.

WEAK VERBS:

The subjunctive has the same forms as the past tense indicative.

Past Indicative	Subjunctive
ich machte	ich machte
du machtest	du machtest

STRONG VERBS, *HABEN, SEIN,* MODALS:

The subjunctive of the verbs in this group has the same endings as the past indicative of weak verbs: **-e, -est, -e, -en, -et, -en** (no **-t-** however). The stem vowel takes an umlaut whenever possible.

Past Indicative	Subjunctive
ich ging	ich ginge
ich gab	ich gäbe
ich hatte	ich hätte
ich war	ich wäre
ich konnte	ich könnte

The modals **wollen** and **sollen** do not take any umlaut so that their subjunctive forms are the same as the past indicative.

There is a strong tendency in German to replace the subjunctive forms with **würde** + infinitive (the exact equivalent of English would + infinitive) in the main clause. In examples A 1-3, German speakers would prefer the **würde**-form to the subjunctive. The subjunctive still holds its place, however, in the **wenn**-clause; **wäre-** and **hätte-** are not replaced by **würde-** forms.

PAST TIME FRAME

1. **Wenn ich (vor einem Jahr) Geld gehabt hätte,**
   (Aber ich hatte kein Geld.)
   If I had had the money,
   (But I did not have the money.)

   hätte ich eine Reise gemacht.

   I would have gone on a trip.

2. **Wenn Erika (gestern) gekommen wäre,**
   (Aber sie kam nicht.)
   If Erika had come yesterday,
   (But she didn't come.)

   hätte ich ein Glas Wein mit ihr getrunken.

   I would have drunk a glass of wine with her.

3. **Wenn du das Auto vor einem Monat von diesem Mann gekauft hättest,**
   (Aber du kauftest es nicht.)
   If you had bought the car from this man a month ago,
   (But you didn't buy it).

   hätte es doppelt so viel gekostet.

   it would have cost twice as much.

All conditions under B refer to situations in the past. They are expressed by the past subjunctive: a form of **hätte** or **wäre** + participle.

KAPITEL 14

PLAYBOY EIN KLUB IN UNSERER STADT?

Debating the possibility of building a Playboy Club in your town is a project that can elicit many realistic as well as fantastic arguments pro and con. The slight frivolity that still surrounds Mr. Hefner's enterprises will rally many forces vehemently opposed to such a plan. Many commercial interests—and others—will support the plan.

What might look like a very difficult and sophisticated task can be handled effectively at this stage of your German studies, if you adjust the rules of the debate for your purposes.

DIE DEBATTE

Personen: **Herr Hefner**
der Bürgermeister	mayor
der Pastor	minister
der Priester	priest
der Architekt	architect
ein Häschen	a bunny
eine "Tochter der	a Daughter of the American
amerikanischen Revolution"	Revolution
der Polizist	policeman
der Heimatdichter	local (regional) poet
eine Feministin	a feminist
der Vorsitzende der	chairman of the chamber of
Handelskammer	commerce
ein Reporter	a reporter

1. Each representative (der Bürgermeister, der Pastor, ein Häschen, etc.) presents his or her case for two to three minutes. New arguments provoked by the first round of statements can be presented in a second round. If a discussion develops among various representatives after the second round, so much the better.
2. Each participant in the debate should prepare a list of words and expressions that may be unknown to the class and are essential for getting the statement across. These words and expressions should be written on the blackboard or mimeographed and distributed to the class before the debate.
3. Several persons may share one role to generate a greater variety of arguments.

A **HERR HEFNER** ist kein Architekt. Aber er weiß, was er will. Hier ist seine Skizze des Playboy Klubs:

After Mr. Hefner has introduced his plan for his new Playboy Club (he should present details in his introduction such as height of building, number of hotel rooms, seating capacity of the restaurant, number of employees, cost, how long it will take to build the club) the participants in the debate should be allowed to ask Mr. Hefner questions concerning the style of the building, whether it will fit in the architecture of the city, how many new jobs the club will create, whether there will be enough parking, how many days per week the club will be open, how late it will be open, etc.

_____

_____

_____

1. ein Landeplatz für
   Hubschrauber°
2. eine "Mondscheinbar"°
3. eine Diskothek
4. ein Restaurant
5. ein Hotel
6. eine Parkgarage
7. Wohnungen für
   die Häschen°
8. die Privatwohnung für
   Herrn Hefner
9. die Einfahrt° zur
   Parkgarage

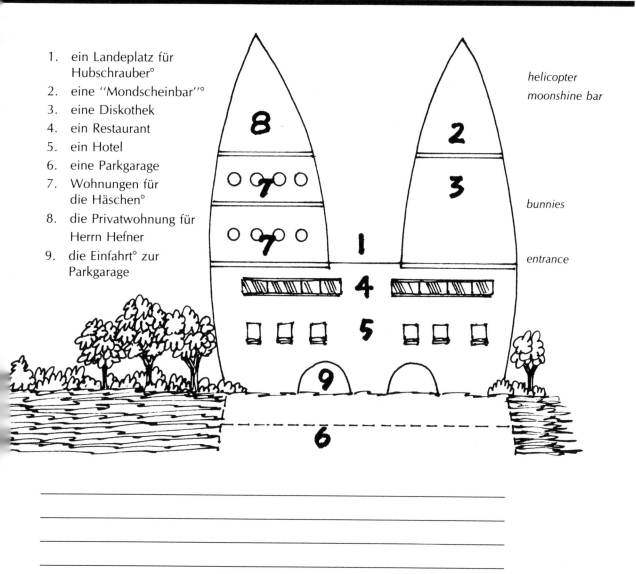

helicopter

moonshine bar

bunnies

entrance

B DER ARCHITEKT

Er kennt Herrn Hefners Skizze. Natürlich muß er versuchen, so zu planen, wie Herr
Hefner es wünscht. Aber er ist der Experte und muß Herrn Hefners Plan kritisieren.
Der Architekt muß sagen was praktisch ist, was unpraktisch ist, was möglich oder
unmöglich ist, was er schön findet, was er nicht so schön findet. Er soll den Plan von
Herrn Hefner verändern° oder seinen eigenen Plan an der Tafel erklären.   *change*
Der Architekt könnte folgende Wörter gebrauchen:

r Bauplatz, ¨-e	building site
s Baumaterial, -ien	building materials
e Baugenehmigung	building permit
s Stockwerk, -e	floor, story
r Beton	.concrete
r Wolkenkratzer, -	skyscraper

C DER PASTOR ODER PRIESTER

The minister's arguments, at the risk of making him a cliché figure, should be apparent: he is against drinking, semi-nude women, the effect of the Playboy Club on the community, especially on the young people. Of course, some daring students could, with good arguments, turn the minister into an advocate of the Playboy Club.
Der Pastor könnte folgende Wörter gebrauchen:

e Moral	morals, morality
e Sünde, -n	sin
in die Kirche gehen	to go to church
im Kirchenchor singen	to sing in the church choir
die Zeit verschwenden	to waste time
ein schlechtes Beispiel geben	to set a bad example

D DER BÜRGERMEISTER

owner
married

Er ist Republikaner und Besitzer° des Hotels "Mayflower," des größten Hotels in der Stadt. Er ist nicht verheiratet.° Er will natürlich, daß es der Stadt gut geht. Der Playboy Klub wäre für sein Hotel keine Konkurrenz. (Of course, you can ignore this background information if you have a different person in mind).

Einige Wörter, die der Bürgermeister gebrauchen könnte:

Steuern *(pl)*	taxes
e Stadtplanung	city planning
e Wirtschaft	economy
e Arbeitslosigkeit	unemployment

_____

_____

_____

_____

_____

E DER HEIMATDICHTER

Er ist alt und liebt seine Stadt so, wie er sie seit seiner Jugend kennt. Er schreibt Gedichte° und Geschichten über die gute alte Zeit. Er ist nicht berühmt°, aber er träumt° davon, einmal berühmt zu werden.

poems
famous
dreams

_____

_____

_____

_____

_____

_____

F When you **DEVELOP THE ARGUMENTS OF THE OTHER PARTICIPANTS**
in the debate, think of their function and what they stand for. A policeman is concerned about people who drink and drive, about parking, traffic, gangsters and

related problems. After work he may very much like to visit the club. A bunny likes the money she is going to make in the club; maybe she hopes to meet a rich man and marry him, or be discovered by a film director. Keep the argument concrete and simple.

G COUNTER THE FOLLOWING ARGUMENTS. Avoid simple negation.

highrise
spoils, corrupts

EXAMPLE: Ein Hochhaus° verdirbt° die Silhouette unserer Stadt.
Ein Hochhaus macht unsere Stadt interessanter.

source of income

1. Der Playboy Klub ist eine gute Einnahmequelle° für die Stadt.

_____

2. Gangster werden in die Stadt kommen.

_____

unemployment
abolished

3. Durch den Playboy Klub wird die Arbeitslosigkeit° beseitigt°.

_____

drunks

4. Mehr Betrunkene° werden in der Stadt Auto fahren.

_____

famous

5. Unsere Stadt wird berühmt° werden.

_____

6. Unsere Stadt wird ihren Charakter verlieren.

_____

leave

7. Die guten Bürger werden die Stadt verlassen.°

_____

8. Filmstars und Politiker werden unsere Stadt besuchen.

_____

9. Wir geben unseren Kindern ein schlechtes Beispiel.

_____

offended

10. Die Frauen in unserer Stadt werden durch einen Playboy Klub beleidigt°.

_____

11. Die Innenstadt wird schöner und interessanter.

_____

mayor

12. Herr Hefner soll unser nächster Bürgermeister° werden.

_____

DIE GESCHICHTE VON ARTHUR UND ALOIS
(Nach einer Fabel von James Thurber)

Es war einmal ein junger Biber.° Er hieß Alois. Da gab es aber auch noch einen *beaver*
anderen Biber, der etwas älter als Alois war. Dieser Biber hieß Arthur. Arthur und
Alois liebten beide dasselbe hübsche° Fräulein. Dieses Fräulein zeigte° Alois, dem *pretty* / *gave the cold shoulder*
jüngeren Biber, die kalte Schulter°, weil er ein Tunichtgut° war. Er hatte in seinem *good-for-nothing*
Leben noch keinen Finger° gerührt°. Denn er zog° es vor,° zu essen, zu trinken, in *lifted a finger* / *preferred*
den Flüssen zu schwimmen und mit den Bibermädchen "Hasch mich"° zu spielen. *catch me*
Arthur, der ältere Biber, hatte dagegen in seinem Leben immer nur gearbeitet. Er fing
schon damit an, als er gerade seine ersten Zähne bekommen hatte. Gespielt hatte er
nie. Eines Tages bat Alois das hübsche Fräulein, ihn zu heiraten. "Das kommt nicht
in Frage," sagte das hübsche Fräulein. "Was bildest° du dir denn ein°? Du hast in *do you think*
deinem Leben noch nichts geleistet." Sie wies darauf hin,° daß Arthur schon *pointed out*
dreiunddreißig Dämme gebaut hatte und an drei weiteren Dämmen arbeitete. Er, Al,
hatte es dagegen in seinem ganzen Leben nicht einmal zu einem Brotbrett° *cutting board*
gebracht.° Das hübsche Fräulein sagte also: "Nein!!" Das tat Alois sehr leid, aber er *acquired*
dachte: "Arbeiten, nur weil eine Frau das will? Das mache ich nicht." Da sagte das
hübsche Fräulein: "Heiraten kann ich dich nicht, aber ich will wie eine Schwester zu
dir sein." Aber Al wies darauf hin, daß er schon siebzehn Schwestern hatte. Also ging
er wieder essen und schlafen, in den Flüssen schwimmen und mit den
Bibermädchen "Hasch mich" spielen. Das hübsche Fräulein aber heiratete Arthur.
Wann? Während der Mittagspause,° denn Arthur konnte nie länger als eine Stunde *lunch break*
freinehmen. Sie hatten sieben Kinder. Arthur arbeitete so schwer für seine Familie,
daß seine Zähne bald nur noch Stummel° waren. Er ruinierte seine Gesundheit° und *stump* / *health*
starb, ohne auch nur einmal in seinem Leben Ferien gemacht zu haben.

Alois aber tat, was er schon immer getan hatte. Er aß und trank, schwamm in den
Flüssen und spielte "Hasch mich" mit den Bibermädchen. Reich geworden ist er
nicht in seinem leben. Aber er amüsierte sich köstlich,° war glücklich und wurde *had great fun*
sehr alt.

Und die Moral von der Geschichte?
Lieber faul und ledig° als fleißig und tot. *single (not married)*

A RETRACE THE STORY with the help of the following cues. Of course, you
need not reproduce each sentence literally. Everybody should contribute at
least one sentence.

Es war einmal...
Da gab es aber auch...
...liebten beide...

...zeigte...die kalte Schuler

...ein Tunichtgut

Alois...keinen Finger...

Denn Alois zog es vor...

Arthur hatte dagegen...

Arthur fing schon damit an, als...

...hatte er nie.

Eines Tages bat Alois...

"..." sagte das hübsche Fräulein. "Was bildest...? Du hast in deinem Leben..."

Sie wies darauf hin, daß Arthur...

Er, Al, hatte es dagegen...

..."Nein!"

Das tat Alois..., aber...

"Arbeiten, nur weil..."

Da sagte das hübsche Fräulein: "Heiraten kann ..., aber ich will..."

Aber Al wies darauf hin, daß...

Also ging er wieder...

Das hübsche Fräulein aber ...

Wann? ...Mittagspause...

...sieben...Arthur arbeitete so schwer..., daß...

Er ruinierte...und starb, ohne...

Alois aber...

Reich geworden...Aber er...

Und die Moral..."..."

B   FRAGEN ÜBER BIBER.

1. Wo leben Biber?

_____

2. Warum gibt es heute nicht mehr so viele Biber?

_____

typical   3. Was ist typisch° für Biber?

_____

4. Warum wählte James Thurber zwei Biber als Protagonisten für seine Fabel?

_____

5. Sind Sie für Alois? Wenn ja, warum?

_____

6. Sind Sie für Arthur? Wenn ja, warum?

_____

C ZWEI MÄNNER LIEBEN DASSELBE MÄDCHEN.

1. Welche Probleme sehen Sie für das Mädchen?

_____

2. Vielleicht gibt es keine Probleme. Warum gibt es keine Probleme?

_____

3. Welche Probleme können für die Männer entstehen?°   _arise_

_____

4. Was machen Sie, wenn Ihnen jemand die kalte Schulter zeigt?

_____

_____

_____

5. Was für einen Mann möchten Sie heiraten?

   Ich möchte einen Mann heiraten, der_____

   der_____

   _____

6. Was für eine Frau möchten Sie heiraten?

   Ich möchte eine Frau heiraten, die_____

   die_____

   _____

7. Wie viele Kinder möchten Sie haben?
   a. vierzehn Kinder
   b. keine Kinder
   c. zwei Kinder
      Explain your choice

_____

_____

_____

D **NAME ANYTHING** that comes to your mind in connection with "schwimmen."

_____

_____

_____

E **FAULENZEN UND ARBEITEN**

good-for-nothing

1. Was tut ein Tunichtgut?°

_____

2. Was tut er nicht?

_____

3. Wenn Sie Sympathien für einen Tunichtgut haben: warum?

_____

4. Ein Leben ohne Arbeit. Was würden Sie tun?

_____

_____

_____

means
to amount to
something

5. Was bedeutet° für Sie: "es im Leben zu etwas bringen"?°

Ich möchte _____

Für mich bedeutet das: _____

_____

ESSENTIAL GRAMMAR: Usage of *Werden*

A WERDEN AS AN AUXILIARY

1. "werden" as auxiliary to form the future tense:

Gangster	**werden** in die Stadt	**kommen.** *(future tense, active)*
form of	**werden +**	**infinitive.**

Gangsters will (are going to) come to the city.

2. "werden" as auxiliary to form the passive voice:

Ein Playboy Klub	**wird** hier	**gebaut.** *(present tense, passive)*
form of	**werden** +	**past participle.**

A Playboy Club is (being) built here.

Ein Playboy Klub	**wurde** hier	**gebaut.** *(past tense, passive)*

A Playboy Club was built here.

Ein Playboy Klub	**ist** hier	**gebaut worden.** *(perfect tense, passive)*

A Playboy Club has been built (was built) here.

B "WERDEN" AS A FULL VERB:

Er wird älter.	He is getting, (becoming, growing) older.	*(present tense)*
Er wird morgen fünfzig.	He is turning fifty tomorrow.	
Er wurde älter.	He grew older	*(past tense)*
Er ist älter geworden.	He has gotten older	*(perfect tense)*

Frequent uses of "werden" as a full verb:

Mein Bruder wird Arzt.	My brother is becoming (studying to be) a doctor.
Mir wird kalt.	I am getting cold.
Mir wird schlecht.	I am getting sick (in the sense of nausea).
Mir wird angst.	I am getting scared.
Das wird nichts.	That's not going to work.

For spoken German, "werden" as a full verb is more important than "werden" as an auxiliary. The passive voice is typical of written German, especially in scientific and technical texts. There is a strong tendency in modern spoken German to use the present tense instead of the future, if an adverb indicates the future or if the future can be assumed from the context: Instead of **Er wird morgen bestimmt kommen** one would normally say **Er kommt morgen bestimmt** or even **Er kommt bestimmt.**

✴ **NOTE:**

1. "werden" as a full verb never takes an accusative object.
   It expresses that *something is happening to a person* (somebody is getting old, becoming a doctor, growing tired, turning fifty, etc.).
2. English "to become" and German "bekommen" are two completely different verbs.
3. "worden" always signals a passive form.
4. "geworden" is always the past participle of "werden" as a full verb.

C **TEST YOUR UNDERSTANDING OF "WERDEN"** by preparing the following questions for the German edition of *Playboy*. Since everybody in class can be expected to impersonate Mr. Hefner, it would be wise to prepare imaginative German answers together with your translation of the questions:

1. Are you going to build a Playboy Club in Leningrad, Mr. Hefner?

   _____

   _____

2. Have you become a millionaire, Mr. Hefner?

   _____

   _____

3. You are getting older, Mr. Hefner, but are you getting wiser?

   _____

   _____

4. What became of your girlfriend Barbie, Mr. Hefner?

   _____

   _____

5. Why do people get sick when reading Playboy jokes, Mr. Hefner?

   _____

   _____

6. When did you turn fifty, Mr. Hefner?

   _____

   _____

7. Did you ever get beaten up (were you ever beaten up) by feminists, Mr. Hefner? When? Where?

8. If not: Why do you never get beaten up by feminists?

9. For how much will your black Playboy plane be sold?

10. Why do you not want to become President of the United States?

11. When are you going to get married?

12. When was your daughter born?

13. What would she like to be?

You will remember Tünnes and Schäl from Chapter 11. Their easy-going approach to life does not allow work to rank high on their scale of values.

Schäl fragt Tünnes: "Wie geht es eigentlich dem Peter? Ich habe ihn lange nicht gesehen."
Tünnes antwortet: "Der arbeitet jetzt."
Da sagt Schäl: "Das ist möglich. Für Geld tut der alles!"

WÖRTERVERZEICHNIS
DEUTSCH-ENGLISCH

A

ab·biegen, bog ab, ist abgebogen to turn off (a road or street)
der Abend, -e evening
das Abendbrot dinner
abends in the evening
aber but
ab·fahren (fährt ab), fuhr ab, ist abgefahren to drive off, leave
ab·nehmen (nimmt ab), nahm ab, abgenommen to lose weight, to decrease, to take off
ab·rüsten to reduce arms, disarm
ab·schalten to switch off
ab·schließen, schloß ab, hat abgeschlossen to lock (door, car etc.)
der Abschluß, ¨-sse conclusion (of schooling, negotiations etc.)
abstrahieren to abstract
die Achse, -n axis, axle
auf der Achse sein (coll.) to be on the move
addieren to add
adoptieren to adopt
der Adoptivvater, ¨-ter adoptive father
aggressiv aggressive
aktiv active
der Alkohol alcohol
allein alone
alles everything
die Alpen (pl.) the Alps
als when, as, than
also therefore, so, well
alt old
der Altar, ¨-e altar

das Altersheim, -e home for the aged, nursing home
das Altwerden growing old
(das) Aluminium aluminum
der Amerikaner, - the American (male)
die Amerikanerin, -nen the American (female)
amerikanisch American
sich amüsieren to enjoy oneself, have fun
an at, on
der Anblick sight, view
ander- other, different
an·fangen (fängt an), fing an, angefangen to begin
an·geben (gibt an), gab an, angegeben to brag
angeln to fish
der (die) Angestellte, -n employee
die Angst, ¨-e anxiety, fear
Angst haben (vor) to be afraid (of)
der Angsthase, -n timid person, "chicken"
ängstlich anxious, timid
an·halten (hält an), hielt an, angehalten to stop
an·kommen, kam an, ist angekommen to arrive
an·nähen to sew on
die Anonymität anonymity
an·rufen, rief an, angerufen to phone, to call (on the phone)
an·schalten to switch on
an·sehen (sieht an), sah an, angesehen to look at
sich einen Film ansehen to

watch a movie
der Antialkoholiker, - teetotaler
die Antilope, -n antelope
die Antwort, -en answer
antworten to answer
an·ziehen, zog an, angezogen to put on, to dress, to attract
sich anziehen to get dressed
der Anzug, ¨-e suit (as a garment)
der Apfel, ¨- apple
die Apotheke, -n pharmacy
der Apotheker, - pharmacist
das Aquarium, Aquarien aquarium
äquivalent equivalent
die Arbeit, -en work, job, paper written in school, college etc.
arbeiten to work
die Arbeitslosigkeit unemployment
der Architekt, -en architect
die Architektur architecture
ärgern to annoy
sich ärgern über to get angry at
das Argument, -e argument
arm poor
der Arm, -e arm
die Armut poverty
arrogant arrogant
der Arzt, ¨-e doctor, physician
die Ärztin, -nen female

doctor
der Ast, -̈e branch
der Athlet, -en athlete
der Atlantik the Atlantic
Ocean
die Atomaufrüstung
nuclear armament
der Atomkrieg, -e nuclear
war
die Atomrakete, -n
nuclear rocket (missile)
auch also, too
auf on, upon, on top of
auf Wiedersehen
good-bye
**auf·bleiben, blieb auf, ist
aufgeblieben** to stay up
(late), to remain open
**auf·essen (ißt auf), aß auf,
aufgegessen** to eat up
die Aufgabe, -n
assignment, task
auf·hören to stop
auf·machen to open
auf·passen to pay
attention, watch out
auf·räumen to clear up, to
put in order
auf·rüsten to arm
**auf·schließen, schloß auf,
aufgeschlossen** to
unlock, open
aufschlußreich informative
auf·setzen to put on
**auf·stehen, stand auf, ist
aufgestanden** to get up
der Aufstieg ascent, rise,
advancement
auf·wachen to wake up
das Auge, -n eye
aus out of, from
**aus·brechen (bricht aus),
brach aus, ist
ausgebrochen** to break
out, erupt
**aus·fliegen, fliegt aus, flog
aus, ist ausgeflogen** to
fly out

**aus·gehen, ging aus, ist
ausgegangen** to go out
ausgerechnet der Chef!
the boss, of all people!
ausgezeichnet excellent
**aus·kommen, kam aus, ist
ausgekommen** to get by,
to manage, to get along
(with)
das Ausland foreign
countries, abroad
**aus·schlafen (schläft aus),
schlief aus,
ausgeschlafen** to sleep
one's fill
**aus·sehen (sieht aus), sah
aus, ausgesehen** to look,
appear
die Außenpolitik foreign
policy
außerdem besides, in
addition
äußerlich external, on the
outside
**aus·steigen, stieg aus, ist
ausgestiegen** to get off
(a vehicle), to get out
der Aussteiger, - drop-out
Australien Australia
**aus·trinken, trank aus,
ausgetrunken** to drink
up
auswendig by heart
auswendig kennen to
know by heart
auswendig lernen to
memorize
**aus·ziehen, zog aus,
ausgezogen** to take off
(clothes), to move out
(of an apartment etc.)
sich ausziehen to undress
das Auto, -s automobile,
car
die Autobahn, -en freeway
**Auto fahren (fährt Auto),
fuhr Auto, ist Auto
gefahren** to drive a car

der Autofahrer, - driver
der Automechaniker, -
auto mechanic

B

das Baby, -s baby, infant
der Bäcker, - baker
die Bäckerei, -en bakery
das Bad, -̈er bath
baden to bathe
die Badewanne, -n bath
tub
das Badezimmer, -
bathroom
der Bahnhof, -̈e railroad
station
bald soon
der Ball, -̈e ball
die Banane, -n banana
die Bank, -̈e bench
die Bank, -en bank
der Bär, -en bear
der Bart, -̈e beard
die Batterie, -n battery
der Bauch, -̈e belly,
stomach
bauen to build
der Bauer, -n farmer
der Baum, -̈e tree
das Baumaterial, -ien
building material
der Bauplatz, -̈e building
site
der Bayer, -n Bavarian
der Beamte, -n official,
civil servant
bedeuten to mean
bedienen to serve
die Bedienung service
sich beeilen to hurry
die Beere, -n berry
bei by, near, with, at
beide both
das Bein, -e leg
beinahe almost, nearly
das Beispiel, -e example
zum Beispiel for example

ein schlechtes Beispiel geben to set a bad example
beißen, biß, gebissen to bite
der Bekannte, -n acquaintance
bekommen, bekam, bekommen to receive, get
beliebt popular
bellen to bark
die Belohnung, -en reward
benutzen to use
das Benzin gasoline
der Berg, -e mountain
bereit prepared, ready
der Bernhardiner, - Saint Bernard
der Beruf, -e profession
berühmt famous
beschreiben to describe
beschützen to protect
beseitigen to abolish
besiegen to defeat
besitzen to own
der Besitzer, - owner
besonders especially
bespritzen to spray
besser better
besser als better than
best- best
(sich) bestellen to order (for oneself)
bestimmt definite
der Besuch, -e visit
besuchen to visit, attend
beten to pray
der Beton concrete
die Betriebswirtschaft business administration
betrunken drunk
der Betrunkene, -n the drunk
das Bett, -en bed
bewachen to guard
sich bewegen to move

bewundern to admire
bezahlen to pay
die Beziehung, -en relationship
der Biber, - beaver
die Bibliothek, -en library
die Biene, -n bee
das Bier, -e beer
das Bild, -er picture
die Bildergeschichte, -n picture story
billig cheap
der Biograph, -en biographer
bis until
bisher up to now
ein bißchen a little bit
bitte please
bitte sehr please
bitten, bat, gebeten to ask
bitten (um) to ask (for)
blau blue
bleiben, blieb, ist geblieben to remain, stay
blitzen to flash
es blitzt there is lightning
der Blödmann, -er moron, "stupid"
das Blut blood
der Boden, - attic
das Bohnenstroh beanstraw
das Boot, -e boat
böse bad, angry, evil
Er ist mir böse. He is angry ("mad") at me.
boxen to box
das Boxen boxing
der Boxer, - boxer
braten (brät), briet, gebraten to roast, to fry
die Bratpfanne, -n frying pan
brauchen to need
braun brown
die Braut, -e bride

der Bräutigam, -e bridegroom
brechen (bricht), brach, gebrochen to break
der Brief, -e letter
breit wide
bremsen to put on the brakes, slow down
die Bremsen (pl.) brakes
die Briefmarke, -n postage stamp
bringen, brachte, gebracht to bring
das Brot, -e bread
das Brotbrett, -er cutting board
das Brötchen, - roll
die Brücke, -n bridge
der Bruder, - brother
das Buch, -er book
der Bundeskanzler, - federal chancellor
der Bürger, - citizen
der Bürgermeister, - mayor
das Büro, -s office
der Bus, -se bus
der Busfahrer, - bus driver
die Butter butter

C

die Chance, -n chance
der Charakter, -e character, nature
der Chef, -s boss, chief, superior
die Chefin, -nen boss *(female)*
die Chemie chemistry
chinesisch Chinese
der Computer, - computer
e Couch, -es couch
der Cousin, -s cousin *(male)*
die Cousine, -n cousin *(female)*

D

da there
dabei while doing it
das Dach, ¨-er roof
dagegen against it
damals then, at that time
die Dame, -n lady
damit with it, by that, thereby, so that
der Damm, ¨-e dam
der Dank thanks, gratitude
danke thank you
danken (+ *dative*) to thank
dann then
darauf on it, then
darüber over it, about that
daß that
dauern to last
davon from it; about it
die Debatte, -n debate
decken to cover
defekt defective
definitiv definite, definitive
dein, deine, dein your (*singular familiar*)
delegieren to delegate
der Demokrat, -en democrat
denken, dachte, gedacht to think
das Denken thinking
der Denker, - thinker
denn for, because
der, die, das the
derselbe, dieselbe, dasselbe, dieselben the same
deswegen for this reason, therefore
deutsch German
der Deutsche, -n German (*male*)
die Deutsche, -n German (*female*)
die Deutschprüfung, -en German test

der Diamant, -en diamond
die Diät diet
der Dichter, - poet
dick fat, thick
der Dienstag Tuesday
dieser, diese, dieses, diese (*pl.*) this, these (*pl.*)
der Diener, - servant
direkt direct
der Diplomat, -en diplomat
die Diskothek, -en discotheque
diskret discreet
diskutieren to discuss
die Disziplin, -en discipline
dividieren to divide
donnern to thunder
der Donnerstag Thursday
die Doppelhochzeit double wedding
doppelt double
das Dorf, ¨-er village
dort there (in that place)
dösen to doze
der Drache, -n dragon
draußen outside
drehen to turn
drinnen inside
drei three
dreimal three times
die Droge, -n drug
der Dschungel jungle
du you (*singular familiar*)
dumm stupid
die Dummheit stupidity
der Dummkopf, ¨-e stupid person
dunkel dark
durch through
dürfen to be permitted, may
durstig thirsty
sich duschen to take a shower, to shower

E

effektiv effective
die Ehe, -n marriage
der Ehemann, ¨-er husband
die Ehescheidung, -en divorce
die Ehrengarde, -n honor guard
das Ei, -er egg
eigen own
eigentlich actually
ein paar a few
einander one another
sich ein·bilden to imagine
einfach simple, easy
die Einfahrt, -en entrance
einig in agreement, unified
ein·laden (lädt ein), lud ein, eingeladen to invite
ein·kaufen to shop
einkaufen gehen to go shopping
die Einkaufstasche, -n shopping bag
einmal once
die Einnahmequelle, -n source of income
einsam lonely
ein·schlafen (schläft ein), ist eingeschlafen to fall asleep
ein·steigen, stieg ein, ist eingestiegen to get into (a vehicle) to board
einzig only
der Einwohner, - resident, inhabitant
das Eis ice, ice cream
das Eisen, - iron
das Eisessen ice cream eating
elegant elegant
der Elektriker, - electrician
elfmal eleven times
eliminieren to eliminate
die Eltern (*pl.*) parents
emanzipiert emancipated

das **Ende, -n** end, conclusion
endlich finally
eng narrow
der **Engel, -** angel
England England
der **Engländer, -** Englishman
die **Engländerin, -nen** Englishwoman
englisch English
der **Enkel, -** grandson
die **Enkelin, -nen** granddaughter
das **Enkelkind, -er** grandchild
entdecken to discover
die **Ente, -n** duck
entfernt far from, distant, away
entgegen·gehen, ging entgegen, ist entgegengegangen to go towards
entlassen (entläßt), entließ, entlassen to fire, dismiss, let go
entstehen, entstand, ist entstanden to originate
enttäuscht disappointed
die **Enttäuschung, -en** disappointment
sich entschuldigen to apologize
sich entspannen to relax
die **Episode, -n** episode
er he
die **Erde** earth
erfahren (erfährt), erfuhr, erfahren to experience, to learn (in the sense of hearing, being informed)
die **Erfahrung, -en** experience
erfinden, erfand, erfunden to invent
der **Erfolg, -e** success
erfolgreich successful

erinnern to remind
sich erinnern to remember
sich erkälten to catch cold
die **Erkältung, -en** cold
erkennen, erkannte, erkannt to recognize
erklären to explain
erlauben to allow, permit
das **Erlebnis, -se** experience (personal)
ernähren to feed, nourish
erst at first, first
ertrinken, ertrank, ist ertrunken to drown
der **Erwachsene, -n** adult
erwarten to expect
erzählen to tell, narrate
die **Erzählung, -en** story, narrative
es it
essen (ißt), aß, gegessen eat (of humans)
das **Essen** food, meal
essengehen, ging essen, ist essengegangen to go to eat
das **Eßzimmer, -** dining room
etwas something
euer, euere, euer your (pl. familiar)
Eulenspiegel ''owl's mirror,'' name of a German prankster and trickster
Europa Europe
die **Existenz, -en** existence
der **Experte, -n** expert
explodieren to explode
exportieren to export

F

die **Fabel, -n** fable, tale
die **Fabrik, -en** factory
das **Fach, -er** subject (such as mathematics, English, etc.)

der **Faden, -** thread, string
fahren (fährt), fuhr, ist gefahren go (in a vehicle), travel, drive
der **Fahrplan, -e** schedule, timetable
das **Fahrrad, -er** bicycle
der **Faktor, -en** factor
fallen (fällt), fiel, ist gefallen to fall
die **Familie, -n** family
das **Familienleben** family life
fangen (fängt), fing, gefangen to catch
die **Farbe, -n** color
der **Faschist, -en** fascist
fast almost
faszinieren to fascinate
faul lazy
faulenzen to be lazy
das **Faultier, -e** sloth
das **Federbett, -en** featherbed, eiderdown comforter
fehlen to be missing, be absent
Er hat uns sehr gefehlt. We missed him very much.
der **Fehler, -** mistake
der **Feierabend, -e** leisure after work
die **Feigheit** cowardice
der **Feigling, -e** coward
das **Fenster, -** window
die **Ferien** (pl.) vacation
der **Fernsehapparat, -e** television set
fern·sehen (sieht fern), sah fern, hat ferngesehen to watch television
das **Fernsehen** television
das **Fernsehprogramm, -e** television program
fertig completed, ready
fesseln to chain, fetter, tie up (prisoners, for

instance)

fest solid, firm

sich festhalten (hält sich fest), hielt sich fest, hat sich festgehalten to hold fast

fett fatty, greasy

das Feuer fire

das Fieber, - fever

der Film, -e film, movie

der Filmjournalist, -en film journalist

der Filmproduzent, -en film producer

der Filmregisseur, -e film director

der Filmstar, -s movie star

die Finanzpolitik financial policy

finden, fand, gefunden to find

der Finger, - finger

die Firma, Firmen company, firm

der Fisch, -e fish

fischen to fish

das Fischgeschäft, -e fish store

die Flasche, -n bottle; slang: poor performer (mainly in athletics)

die Fledermaus, -̈e bat (animal)

fleißig industrious

fliegen, flog, ist geflogen to fly

der Flieger, - flier, pilot

fließen, floß, ist geflossen to flow, run

der Fluch, -̈e curse

der Flügel, - wing

der Flughafen, -̈en airport

die Flugstunde, -n flying lesson

das Flugzeug, -e airplane

der Fluß, Flüsse river

folgend following

fort away

fortgehen, ging fort, ist fortgegangen to go away

die Fortsetzung, -en continuation, sequel

die Fracht, -en freight, cargo

der Frachter, - freighter

die Frage, -n question

fragen to ask

der Fragebogen, -̈ questionnaire

Frankreich France

der Franzose, -n Frenchman

die Französin, -nen Frenchwoman

französisch French

die Frau, -en woman

das Fräulein, - young lady

frei·nehmen to take a day off

der Freitag Friday

die Freizeit free time, leisure

die Fremdenlegion foreign legion

der Fremdenlegionär, -e foreign legionary

fressen (frißt), fraß, gefressen to eat (of animals)

die Freude, -n joy, pleasure

sich freuen to be happy, pleased

sich freuen auf to look forward to

der Freund, -e friend, male friend

die Freundin, -nen friend, female friend

freundlich friendly

die Freundschaft, -en friendship

frieren, fror, gefroren to freeze

frisch fresh

der Friseur, -e barber, hairdresser

froh glad, happy

der Frosch, -̈e frog; slang: "chicken" (timid person)

der Froschschenkel, - frog's leg

früh early

der Frühling, -e spring

das Frühstück breakfast

(sich) fühlen to feel

führen to lead

fünf five

fünfmal five times

funken to radio

funktionieren to function

für for

fürchten to fear

sich fürchten vor to be afraid of

der Fuß, -̈e foot

zu Fuß on foot

der Fußball, -̈e soccer, soccerball

der Fußballplatz, -̈e soccer field

der Fußballspieler soccer player (male)

die Fußballspielerin, -nen soccer player (female)

füttern to feed (animals)

G

der Gangster, - gangster

ganz whole, complete, quite

die Garage, -n garage

die Gardine, -n curtain

der Garten, - garden

das Gasthaus, -̈er inn

die Gastwirtschaft, -en restaurant, inn

geben (gibt), gab, gegeben to give

das Gebiß, Gebisse false teeth, set of teeth

gebrauchen to use

der Geburtstag, -e
birthday
die Geburtstagstorte, -n
birthday cake
der Gedanke, -n thought
das Gedicht, -e poem
die Gefahr, -en danger
gefährlich dangerous
gefallen (gefällt), gefiel,
gefallen to please
das Gefängnis, -se prison
gegen against
gegenüber·stehen, stand
gegenüber,
gegenübergestanden to
stand opposite
gehen, ging, ist gegangen
to walk
Wie geht es Ihnen? How
are you?
gehören to belong to
geistig mental, spiritual
das Geld, -er money
gelingen, gelang, ist
gelungen to succeed
gemütlich cozy,
good-natured
genau exact, precise
genauso just as
genießen, genoß, genossen
to enjoy
genug enough
gerade straight, just
gerecht fair, just
gern (plus verb) to like
das Geschäft, -e business,
store
geschehen, (geschieht),
geschah, ist geschehen
to happen
die Geschichte, -n story,
history
der Geschmack, -er taste,
flavor, good taste
das Geschrei shouting,
outcry
die Gesellschaft, -en
society

das Gesetz, -e law
das Gesicht, -er face,
vision
das Gespräch, -e
conversation
gestern yesterday
gestiefelt booted, in boots
gesund healthy
die Gesundheit health
die Gewerkschaft, -en
trade union
das Gewicht, -e weight
gewinnen, gewann,
gewonnen to win
das Gewissen, -
conscience
gewöhnlich usual,
ordinary
gießen, goß, gegossen to
pour
der Gips, - plaster of Paris,
plaster cast
die Gitarre, -n guitar
das Glas, -er glass,
drinking glass
glauben to believe
glauben an to believe in
gleich same, alike;
immediately, at once
das Gleis, -e track (of
railroad)
gleiten, glitt, ist geglitten
to glide, slide
das Glück good luck,
happiness
glücklich happy
das Gold gold
der Goldfisch, -e goldfish
der Goldhamster, - gold
hamster
die Goldmedaille, -n gold
medal
das Goldstück, -e gold
piece
der Gott, -er God; god
das Gras, -er grass
der Grieche, -n Greek
groß large, big, tall

grün green
der Grund, -e ground,
soil; reason
der Gründer, - founder
gründlich thorough
die Gruppe, -n group
der Gruß, -e greeting
garantiert guaranteed
gut good, well
so gut wie as good as, as
well as
der Gummi gum, rubber
der Gürtel, - belt

H

das Haar, -e hair
haben (hat), hatte, gehabt
to have
halbnackt half-naked
halten (hält), hielt,
gehalten to stop, hold
halten von to feel about,
have an opinion of
halten für to consider,
regard as
der Hamburger, -
hamburger
der Hamster, - hamster
die Hand, -e hand
hängen (hängt), hing,
gehangen (intransitive)
to hang
die Handelskammer, -n
Chamber of Commerce
der Handschlag, -e
handshake
hart hard, difficult, harsh
"Hasch mich" "catch me"
das Häschen, - bunny
hassen to hate
häßlich ugly, nasty
die Hauptrolle, -n leading
role
die Hauptstadt, -e capital
(city)
das Haus, -er house
nach Hause gehen to go

home
zu Haus(e) at home
die Hausaufgabe, -n homework
der Haushalt, -e household
das Haustier, -e pet
die Haustür, -en front door
heben, hob, gehoben to lift, raise
heilig holy
die Heimat home, homeland
der Heimatdichter, - local (regional) poet
heiraten to marry
heiß hot
heißen, hieß, geheißen to be called (by a name)
der Held, -en hero
die Heldin, -nen heroine
helfen (hilft), half, geholfen to help
das Hemd, -en shirt
der Herbst fall, autumn
her·kommen, kam her, ist hergekommen to come here
das Heroin heroin
der Herr, -en gentleman
herrlich splendid, grand
her·stellen to manufacture, produce
herzlich hearty, sincere
heute today
heute abend this evening
hier here
die Hilfe help, aid
der Himmel, - sky, heaven
hin- und her·schaukeln to rock back and forth
hinauf·gehen, ging hinauf, ist hinaufgegangen to go up
hinein·gehen to go in
hin·fahren (fährt hin), fuhr hin, ist hingefahren to drive there
hinter behind
hinunter·fallen, fiel hinunter, ist hinuntergefallen to fall down
hinunter·gehen, ging hinunter, ist hinuntergegangen to go or walk down
der Hinweis, -e indication, allusion, hint
hin·weisen, wies hin, hingewiesen to point to, point out
das Hobby, -s hobby
hoch high
das Hochhaus, ¨-er high-rise, skyscraper
die Hochzeit, -en wedding
die Hochzeitsnacht, ¨-e wedding night
hoffen to hope
die Höhe, -n height, altitude
der Höhepunkt, -e high point, climax
holen to fetch, go for
der Holländer, - Dutchman, the Dutch
die Holländerin, -nen Dutchwoman
das Holz, ¨-er wood
der Honig honey
hören to hear, listen
die Hornhaut callus, horny skin
die Hose, -n pants, trousers
das Hotel, -s hotel
hübsch pretty, beautiful, handsome, good-looking
der Hubschrauber, - helicopter
das Huhn, ¨-er hen, chicken
der Humor humor
der Hund, -e dog
hundert hundred
hupen to honk

I

ich I
die Idee, -n idea
identifizieren to identify
der Idiot, -en idiot
idiotisch idiotic
ihm (to) him
ihn him
ihnen (to) them
Ihnen (to) you *(formal, singular and plural)*
ihr you *(2nd person plural familiar)*; (to) her; their
Ihr your *(formal, singular and plural)*
imitieren to imitate
immer always
importieren to import
improvisieren to improvise
individuell individual
die Inflation inflation
informieren to inform
die Inkakultur Inca culture
das Inland home (native) country as opposed to abroad (foreign country)
die Innenpolitik domestic policy
die Innenstadt, ¨-e (inner) city
innerlich inner, inward
das Insekt, -en insect
die Insel, -n island
intelligent intelligent
die Intelligenz intelligence
der Intelligenzquotient, -en intelligence quotient
intensiv intensive
interessant interesting
sich interessieren (für) to be interested (in)
das Interview, -s interview
inzwischen in the meantime

irgendein, -e some, any
irgendwo somewhere, anywhere
Italien Italy
der Italiener, - Italian
die Italienerin, -nen Italian (woman)
italienisch Italian

J

ja yes
die Jacke, -n jacket, coat
das Jackett, -s jacket, short coat
die Jagd, -en the hunt
jagen to hunt
das Jahr, -e year
das Jahrhundert, -e century
jeder, -e, -es each
jedenfalls in any case
jemand someone
jene that, those
jetzt now, at present
joggen to jog
die Jugend youth; young people
jung young
der Junge, -n boy

K

das Kabelprogramm, -e cable program
der Käfer, - beetle
der Kaffee coffee
die Kaffeekanne, -n coffee pot
das Kaffeetrinken drinking coffee
der Kaiser, - emperor
kalt cold
sich kämmen to comb one's hair
der Kampf, -̈e fight
kämpfen to fight
der Kämpfer, - fighter

das Kreuz, -e cross
der Kanzler, - chancellor
der Kapitalismus capitalism
der Kapitalist, -en capitalist
kaputt ruined, broken (down)
die Karriere, -n career
die Karte, -n card
Karten spielen to play cards
die Kartoffel, -n potato
der Kartoffelesser one who eats potatoes
der Käse cheese
der Kater, - tomcat
der Katholik, -en Catholic
die Katze, -n cat
kauen to chew
kaufen to buy
das Kaufhaus, -̈er department store
der Kaufmann, Kaufleute businessman
der Kaugummi chewing gum
das Kaugummikauen gum chewing
kein, -e, - no, not a
der Keller, - cellar, basement
kennen, kannte, gekannt to be acquainted with
kennen·lernen to become acquainted
kentern to capsize
die Kettenreaktion, -en chain reaction
der/das Kilometer, - kilometer
das Kind, -er child
das Kinderzimmer, - children's room
das Kino, -s movie theater
die Kirche, -n church
der Kirchenchor, -̈e church choir

die Kiste, -n box, chest
der Klang, -̈e sound
die Klappe, -n flap
klar clear
die Klasse, -n class
der Klassenkamerad, -en classmate
klassisch classic
der Klatsch gossip
klatschen to applaud
das Klavier, -e piano
kleben to stick
das Kleid, -er dress, clothes
die Kleidung clothing
klein small
klettern to climb
klingeln to ring
klingen, klang, geklungen to sound
das Klischee, -s cliché
klopfen to knock
der Klub, -s club
klug bright, intelligent
der Klugscheißer, - "clever-shitter"; know-it-all, wise guy
der Knall, -e crack, pop, bang, explosion
Du hast einen Knall. You are crazy.
die Kneipe, -n tavern, "dive"
der Knochen, - bone
der Knopf, -̈e button, knob
kochen to cook, to boil
das Kofferradio, -s portable radio
der Kofferraum, -̈e trunk (of a car)
der Kollege, -n colleague (male)
die Kollegin, -nen colleague (female)
komisch comical, peculiar, strange
kommen, kam, ist gekommen to come

zu spät kommen to come late

Es kommt darauf an. It depends.

der Kommentar, -e commentary

der Kommunist, -en communist

kommunistisch communist

kompensieren to compensate

die Konditorei, -en pastry shop, bakery and café in one

der König, -e king

die Königin, -nen queen

die Konkurrenz, -en competition

können to be able to

sich konzentrieren to concentrate

konzentriert concentrated

das Konzert, -e concert

der Kopf, -̈e head

kopieren to copy

das Konto, die Konten account

der Korb, -̈e basket

korrespondieren to correspond

kosten to cost

köstlich delightful

krank sick

das Krankenhaus, -̈er hospital

kreativ creative

kriechen, kroch, ist gekrochen to crawl

der Krieg, -e war

kritisch critical

kritisieren to criticize

die Küche, -n kitchen

der Kuchen, - cake, pastry

die Kugel, -n bullet, ball, shot

das Kugelstoßen shotput

kühlen to cool

der Kühler, - radiator (of car)

der Kühlschrank, -̈e refrigerator

der Kunde, -n customer

die Kupplung clutch

der Kurs, -e course

kurz short

die Kurzgeschichte, -n short story

L

lächeln to smile

lächelnd smiling

lachen to laugh

das Land, -̈er land, country

landen to land

der Landeplatz, -̈e landing pad

lang long

langsam slow, slowly

die Langeweile boredom

langweilig boring

lassen (läßt), ließ, gelassen let, leave

das Lasso, -s lasso

laufen (läuft), lief, ist gelaufen to run, walk

die Laune, -n mood

laut loud

leben to live

das Leben life

die Lederhose, -n leather shorts or pants

ledig single (unmarried)

legen to lay, put, set

lehren to teach

der Lehrer, - teacher

die Lehrerin, -nen teacher (female)

leicht light, easy

das Leid pain

Es tut mir leid. I'm sorry.

leider unfortunately

leihen, lieh, geliehen to loan (money), to borrow

leisten to accomplish, achieve

lernen to learn

lesen (liest), las, gelesen to read

letzt- last

die Leute (pl.) people

das Licht, -er light

lieb dear

lieben to love

lieber als (rather) better . . . than

die Liebesgeschichte, -n love story

der Liebesroman, -e love story (novel)

liegen, lag, gelegen to lie, to be situated

der Likör, -e liqueur

die Limousine, -n limousine

das Lindenblatt, -̈er leaf of a linden tree

links to the left

der/das Liter, - liter

die Literatur, -en literature

loben to praise

das Loch, -̈er hole

der Lockenwickler, - hair curler

los loose, free

Was ist los? What's the matter?

lösen to solve

los·fahren (fährt los), fuhr los, ist losgefahren to drive off, set out, depart

der Löwe, -n lion

die Luft, -̈e air

die Lüge, -n lie, untruth

lügen, log, gelogen to lie, to tell a lie

die Lust, -̈e pleasure, delight

Lust haben to be inclined, want to do something

M

machen to make, do
das Mädchen, - girl
der Maikäfer, - May beetle, May bug
der Mais corn
der Maler, - painter, artist
man one, you (people)
manch, manche many a, some
manchmal sometimes
der Mann, ¨-er man
männlich male, manly
der Mantel, ¨- overcoat
das Marathon marathon
das Märchen, - fairy-tale
marinieren to marinate
marschieren to march
materialistisch materialistic
die Mathematik mathematics
die Mauer, -n wall
die Mauerschwalbe, -n swallow
die Maus, ¨-e mouse
die Medizin, -en medicine
das Meer, -e sea, ocean
mehr more
mehr als more than
mehrere several
die Meile, -n mile
mein my
meinen to be of the opinion, to mean
die Meinung, -en opinion
meistens mostly
der Mensch, -en person, man (as a species), (pl. people)
merken to notice
der/das Meter meter
die Methode, -n method
mieten to rent, to hire
die Milch milk
der Millionär, -e millionaire

militaristisch militaristic
mindestens at (the) least
die Minute, -n minute
mir (to) me
mißtrauisch distrustful, suspicious
mit with
mit·nehmen (nimmt mit), nahm mit, mitgenommen to take (along) with
der Mittag, -e midday, noon
das Mittagessen, - lunch
die Mittagspause, -n lunch break
das Mittelmeer Mediterranean Sea
mitten (in) in the middle (of)
der Mittwoch Wednesday
mögen to like to
möglich possible
die Möglichkeit, -en possibility
der Moment, -e moment
der Monarchist, -en monarchist
der Mond, -e moon
die Mondscheinbar moonshine bar
der Montag Monday
die Moral moral, "lesson"; morals, ethics
der Mord, -e murder
der Morgen, - morning
morgen tomorrow
der Morgenrock, ¨-e dressing gown, robe
die Morgenstunde, -n morning hours
das Motorrad, ¨-er motor cycle
das Motto, -s motto
müde tired
die Mühle, -n mill
der Müller, - miller
multiplizieren to multiply

(mathematics)
der Mund, ¨-er mouth
das Museum, die Museen museum
die Musik music
das Musikkorps band
müssen to have to
mutig brave, courageous
die Mutter, ¨- mother
die Mütze, -n cap
mythisch mythical
die Mythologie, -n mythology
der Mythos, die Mythen myth

N

nach after, to
der Nachbar, -n neighbor
nach·denken, dachte nach, nachgedacht to think (over), reflect, ponder
nach·kommen, kam nach, ist nachgekommen to come after, follow
nach·laufen (läuft nach), lief nach, ist nachgelaufen follow, run after
der Nachmittag, -e afternoon
die Nachricht, -en news
nach·sehen (sieht nach), sah nach, nachgesehen to check, look up
nächst- next
die Nacht, ¨-e night
der Nachteil, -e disadvantage
nach·zählen to count again
die Nadel, -n needle, pin
der Nagel, - nail
die Naht, ¨-e seam
der Name, -n name
der Narr, -en fool
die Nase, -n nose

der Nationalismus
nationalism
die Natur, -en nature,
temperament
der Naturfreund, -e nature
lover
natürlich natural, naturally
navigieren to navigate
neben beside, by
nebenan next-door, close
by
**nehmen (nimmt), nahm,
genommen** to take
neidisch envious
nein no
nervös nervous
nett nice, pleasant
neu new
neugierig curious
nicht not
der Nichtraucher, -
non-smoker
nichts nothing
nie never
niedlich cute, pretty
niemand nobody, no one
die Niete, -n lottery blank
slang: loser
noch still, yet
nochmals once more
der Nordpol North Pole
nötig necessary
der Nudist, -en nudist
nur only
nutzen to use, utilize

O

ob if, whether
die Oberschule, -n high
school
obwohl although
der Ofen, - stove, oven
offen open
öffnen to open
oft often
ohne without
ohnmächtig fainting, in a

faint
das Öl, -e oil
der Ölwechsel oil change
der Olympiasieger, -
olympic winner, olympic
champion
olympisch olympic
die Olympischen Spiele
the Olympic Games
die Oma, -s grandma
der Onkel, - uncle
der Opa, -s grandpa
die Oper, -n opera
optimistisch optimistic
der Orangensaft, -e
orange juice
die Ordnung, -en order
die Orgel, -n organ
(musical)
originell original

P

das Paar, -e pair, couple
Papi Daddy
der Papst, -e pope
der Park, -s park
die Parkgarage, -n parking
garage
der Parkplatz, -e parking
place, parking lot
der Partner, - partner
(male)
die Partnerin, -nen partner
(female)
passen to fit
passieren to happen
der Pastor, -en pastor,
clergyman
pensioniert retired,
''pensioned''
die Person, -en person
persönlich personal
pessimistisch pessimistic
die Pfeife, -n pipe, whistle
das Pferd, -e horse
das Pfund, -e pound
phantastisch phantastic,

terrific
die Philosophie, -n
philosophy
der Photograph, -en
photographer
photographieren to
photograph
die Physik physics
das Picknick, -s picnic
piepen to chirp
die Pille, -n pill
der Pilot, -en pilot *(male)*
die Pilotin, -nen pilot
(female)
der Plan, -e plan
planen to plan
der Planet, -en planet
Plastik plastic (material)
platt flat, flattened
die Platte, -n record;
platter
platzen to burst, explode
plötzlich suddenly
die Politik politics
der Politiker, - politician
die Polizei police
der Polizist, -en
policeman
populär popular
die Popularität popularity
die Post post office, mail
prachtvoll magnificent
prahlen to boast, show off
praktisch practical
der Präsident, -en
president *(male)*
die Präsidentin, -nen
president *(female)*
präzis exact, precise
der Preis, -e price, prize
die Presse the press
der Pressephotograph, -en
press photographer
der Preuße, -n the
Prussian
der Priester, - priest
die Privatwohnung, -en
private apartment

pro per
probieren to test, try
das Problem, -e problem
problematisch problematic
das Produkt, -e product
produzieren to produce
der Professor, -en
professor *(male)*
die Professorin, -nen
professor *(female)*
der Profi, -s professional
athlete
programmieren to
program
propagieren to propagate
der Protest, -e protest
protestieren to protest
provozierend provocative
die Prüfung, -en test,
exam
das Publikum the public
der Pudel, - poodle
der Pullover, - sweater
putzen to clean, polish
sich die Zähne putzen to
brush one's teeth

Q

qualifizieren to qualify
die Quelle, -n spring,
fountain, source
quitt sein to be even, not
owe anything

R

der Rabe, -n raven
die Rache revenge
rad·fahren (fährt Rad),
fuhr Rad, ist
radgefahren to ride a
bike
das Radio, -s radio
die Rakete, -n rocket
sich rasieren to shave
ratifizieren to ratify
die Ratte, -n rat

der Rauch smoke
rauchen to smoke
der Raucher, - smoker
die Raumkapsel, -n space
capsule
raus out
das Rauschgift, -e drug,
dope
reagieren to react
realistisch realistic
rebellieren to rebel
der Rechtsanwalt, ̈-e
lawyer *(male)*
die Rechtsanwältin, -nen
lawyer *(female)*
die Rede, -n speech
reden to talk
eine Rede halten (hält),
hielt, gehalten to give a
speech
die Redewendung, -en
phrase
der Regenmantel, ̈-
raincoat
der Regenschirm, -e
umbrella
regnen to rain
reich rich
der Reichtum, ̈-er wealth,
fortune
die Reise, -n trip
reisen to travel
reiten, ritt, geritten to
ride, go on horseback
die Reklame, -n
advertisement
der Rekord, -e record
reparieren to repair
der Reporter, - reporter
der Republikaner, -
republican
respektieren to respect
der Rest, -e rest,
remainder, leftovers (of a
meal)
das Restaurant, -s
restaurant
das Resultat, -e result

das Resümee, -s resumé
retten to rescue
die Revolution, -en
revolution
der Revolver, - revolver
richtig correct, right
riechen, roch, gerochen to
smell, sniff
das Rind, -er cow
der Ring, -e ring
die Rolle, -n role, part;
roll, cylinder
die Rose, -n rose
rot red
der Rücken, - back
rufen, rief, gerufen to call,
call out
die Ruhe rest, quiet
ruhig quiet
ruinieren to ruin
rund round
der Russe, -n Russian
Rußland Russia

S

der Sabotageakt, -e act of
sabotage
sagen to say, tell
sammeln to gather, collect
der Samstag Saturday
der Sand sand
der Sänger, - singer
die Sau, ̈-e sow, swine
das Sauerkraut sauerkraut
der Säufer, - drunkard
(male)
die Säuferin, -nen
drunkard *(female)*
schade what a pity, too
bad
schaden to hurt, damage
das Schaf, -e sheep
schaffen, schuf, geschaffen
to create
die Schallplatte, -n
phonograph record
schalten to govern,

operate

sich schämen to feel ashamed

schätzen guess

schauen to look

der Schauspieler, - actor

die Schauspielerin, -nen actress

der Schauspielunterricht acting lessons

scheinen, schien, geschienen to shine, to seem

schenken to give, make a present of

schicken to send

schießen, schoß, geschossen to shoot

das Schießpulver gunpowder

das Schiff, -e ship

schimpfen to insult, grumble

der Schlaf sleep

schlafen (schläft), schlief, geschlafen to sleep

schlafen gehen to go to sleep

das Schlafzimmer, - bedroom

schlagen (schlägt), schlug, geschlagen to hit, beat

die Schlagsahne whipped cream

die Schlange, -n snake

der Schlauberger, - Mr. Clever, know-it-all

schließen, schloß, geschlossen to shut

schlecht bad

schleppen to drag, tow, struggle, be burdened

der Schlüssel, - key

schmecken to taste

der Schmerz, -en pain, ache

der Schmetterling, -e butterfly

sich schminken to make up one's face

schmutzig dirty

der Schnabel, - bill, beak

der Schnee snow

der Schneider, - tailor

schneien to snow

schnell quick, rapid, fast, quickly

die Schnellreinigung, -en fast dry-cleaning

schon already

schön pretty, beautiful

der Schönheitssalon, -s beauty parlor

der Schönheitswettbewerb, -e beauty contest

der Schrank, - cupboard, closet

die Schraube, -n screw

der Schreck shock, fear, alarm

schreiben, schrieb, geschrieben to write

das Schreiben writing

schreien, schrie, geschrien to cry out, scream

der Schriftsteller, - author *(male)*

die Schriftstellerin, -nen author *(female)*

der Schritt, -e step

der Schuh, -e shoe

schuld haben to be guilty

schuldig guilty

die Schule, -n school

der Schüler, - pupil

die Schulter, -n shoulder

schütteln to shake

schützen to protect

schwach weak

die Schwäche, -n weakness

der Schwanz, -e tail

schwarz black

Schwarzwälder Kirschtorte Black Forest Cherry cake

Schweden Sweden

das Schweigen silence

das Schwein, -e hog, pig

die Schweinerei, -en "mess"

die Schweiz Switzerland

schwer hard, difficult, heavy

das Schwergewicht, -e heavyweight

das Schwert, -er sword

die Schwester, -n sister

das Schwimmbad, -er swimming pool

schwimmen, schwamm, ist geschwommen to swim

schwimmen gehen to go swimming

der Schwimmer, - swimmer

die Schwimmhalle, -n indoor pool

die Schwimmweste, -n life jacket

sechs six

sechzehn sixteen

sechzig sixty

der See, -n lake

die See ocean

segeln to sail

der Segen, - blessing

sehen (sieht), sah, gesehen to see

sehr very

das Seil, -e rope

sein (ist), war, ist gewesen to be, exist

sein his, its

seit since

die Seite, -n side; page

die Sekunde, -n second

selbst self, in person

senden to send, dispatch

sentimental sentimental

die Serie, -n series

der Sessel, - easy chair

setzen to place, put

sich setzen to sit down

die **Show, -s** show
sicher safe
sie she, they
Sie you (formal, singular, plural)
siehe see (imperative)
das **Silber** silver
die **Silhouette, -n** silhouette
singen, sang, gesungen to sing
die **Situation, -en** situation
sitzen, saß, gesessen to sit
ski·laufen to ski
die **Skizze, -n** sketch
der **Skrupel, -** scruple
das **Sofa, -s** sofa
sofort immediately
sogar even
der **Sohn, ⸚e** son
solange as long as
solch such
sollen ought to, should
der **Sommer** summer
sondern but (on the contrary)
der **Sonnabend, -e** Saturday
die **Sonne, -n** sun
der **Sonnenschirm, -e** sunshade
das **Sonnenöl, -e** sun-tan oil
der **Sonntag, -e** Sunday
sonstwo elsewhere
sooft as often (as)
die **Sorge, -n** worry
Machen Sie sich keine Sorgen. Don't worry.
das **Souvenir, -s** souvenir
soviel as much
der **Sowjet, -s** Soviet
der **Sozialismus** socialism
der **Sozialist, -en** socialist
der **Spanier, -** Spaniard (male)
die **Spanierin, -nen** Spaniard (female)

spannend exciting, suspenseful
sparen to save (money)
der **Spaß, ⸚e** fun
zum Spaß for fun
später later
spazieren·gehen, ging spazieren, ist spazierengegangen to go for a walk
der **Speer, -e** spear, javelin
der **Speerwurf, ⸚e** javelin throw
die **Spekulation, -en** speculation
der **Spiegel, -** mirror
das **Spiegelei, -er** fried egg (sunny-side-up)
das **Spiel, -e** play, game
spielen to play
die **Speisekarte, -n** menu
die **Spinne, -n** spider
spinnen, spann, gesponnen to spin; to make up stories
der **Spion, -e** spy
der **Spitzname, -n** nickname
der **Sport** sport
der **Sportler, -** athlete
sportlich sporting, athletic
die **Sprache, -n** language
sprechen (spricht), sprach, gesprochen to talk
das **Sprichwort, ⸚er** proverb
springen, sprang, ist gesprungen to jump
spritzen to spray, squirt
der **Staat, -en** state, country
der **Staatsbesuch, -e** state visit
das **Stadion, Stadien** stadium
die **Stadt, ⸚e** city
die **Stadtplanung** city planning

der **Stahl** steel
der **Stamm, ⸚e** trunk, stem
stammen (von) to originate, to descend (from)
stark strong
die **Stärke, -n** strength
stechen (sticht), stach, gestochen to sting
stecken to put; to stick
stehen, stand, gestanden to stand
stehlen (stiehlt), stahl, gestohlen to steal
steil steep
die **Stelle, -n** place, position
stellen to put, place
sterben (stirbt), starb, ist gestorben to die
das **Stereotyp, -en** stereotype
das **Steuer, -** steering wheel
die **Steuern** (pl.) taxes
die **Stewardeß, -(ss)en** stewardess
der **Stil, -e** style
die **Stimme, -n** voice, vote
stimmen to be correct
der **Stock, ⸚e** stick; floor (story in a building)
das **Stockwerk, -e** floor, story
stolz proud
stopfen to stuff
stoppen to stop
stören to disturb
stoßen (stößt), stieß, gestoßen to push, shove
die **Strafe, -n** punishment, penalty
der **Strand, ⸚e** beach, shore
die **Straße, -n** street
der **Streich, -e** trick, prank
streicheln to stroke, pet
das **Streichholz, ⸚er** match

(for lighting)
streiken to strike
die Strömung, -en current, stream
der Student, -en student (male)
die Studentin, -nen student (female)
studieren to study
der Stummel, - stump, stub
die Stunde, -n hour
stützen to support
suchen to seek
der Südpol South Pole
die Sünde, -n sin
der Superlativ, -e superlative
der Supermarkt, -̈e super market
süß sweet
die Sympathie, -n sympathy
sympathisch likeable, congenial
das System, -e system
die Szene, -n scene

T

die Tafel, -n board, blackboard
der Tag, -e day
Guten Tag! Hello, good day
tanken to refuel, fill up
die Tankstelle, -n gas station
die Tante, -n aunt
tanzen to dance
der Tänzer, - dancer (male)
die Tänzerin, -nen dancer (female)
die Tanzfläche, -n dance floor
die Tanzszene, -n dance scene

die Tasche, -n pocket
die Tarnkappe, -n cloak of invisibility
die Tasse, -n cup
der Tausendfüßler, - centipede
der Taxifahrer, - taxi driver
der Tee tea
der Teenager, - teenager
telefonieren to telephone
die Telefonrechnung, -en telephone bill
telegraphieren to telegraph
der Teller, - plate, dish
der Teppich, -e carpet
die Terrasse, -n terrace
der Terrorist, -en terrorist
teuer expensive
der Teufel, - devil
das Theater, - theater
die Theorie, -n theory
tief deep
der Tiefflieger, - low flying aircraft, strafer
das Tier, -e animal
der Tierarzt, -̈e veterinarian
der Tierfreund, -e animal lover
der Tiger, - tiger
tippen to type
der Tisch, -e table
die Tochter, -̈ daughter
der Tod, -e death
toll terrific, ''great''
das Tonband, -̈er tape (recording)
das Tor, -e goal, gate, door
tot dead
töten to kill
der Tourist, -en tourist
die Touristeninsel, -n tourist island
traditionell traditional
tragen (trägt), trug,

getragen to carry; wear
trainieren to coach, train, exercise
der Traum, -̈e dream
träumen to dream
traurig sad
treffen (trifft), traf, getroffen to meet
treiben, trieb, getrieben to drive
die Treppe, -n stairway
trinken, trank, getrunken to drink
der Tropenhelm, -e sun helmet, tropical helmet
trotzdem in spite of it, nevertheless
tun, tat, getan to do
der Tunichtgut, -e good-for-nothing
die Tür, -en door
der Typ, -en type, model
typisch typical
tyrannisieren to tyrannize

U

u.s.w. (und so weiter) and so on, et cetera
über over, above, about
überall everywhere
überholen overtake
über Nacht overnight
übernachten to stay overnight
übrig left over, remaining
übrigens by the way
das Ufer, - shore
die Uhr, -en clock, o'clock
Wieviel Uhr ist es? What time is it?
um around, about; in order to
um·fallen (fällt um), fiel um, ist umgefallen to fall over
unabhängig independent

unbedingt unconditional;
  by all means
unbekannt unknown
und and
der Unfall, -̈e accident
die Unfallstelle, -n scene
  of an accident
ungebildet uneducated
das Unglück misfortune
der Unglücksrabe, -n
  unfortunate raven
die Uni, -s university
die Universität, -en
  university
unmöglich impossible
unmoralisch immoral
unorthodox unorthodox
unpraktisch impractical
unrealistisch unrealistic
uns us
unschädlich harmless
unser our
unsichtbar invisible
der Unsinn nonsense
unsympathisch unpleasant
unter under
umterhalten (unterhält),
  unterhielt, unterhalten
  to support, entertain
sich unterhalten to
  converse
der Unterricht instruction,
  lessons
unterrichten to teach, to
  instruct
die Unterseite, -n
  underside
unverwundbar
  invulnerable
unterwegs on the way, en
  route
der Urlaub vacation, leave

V

der Vater, -̈ father
ventilieren to ventilate
sich verabreden make an

appointment
die Verabredung, -en
  appointment, date
verändern to change
verbinden, verband,
  verbunden to join,
  unite, tie together
der Verbrecher, - criminal
verbringen, verbrachte,
  verbracht to spend
  (time)
verderben (verdirbt),
  verdarb, verdorben to
  spoil, corrupt
verdienen to earn
die Vereinigten Staaten
  the United States
verführerisch seductive
die Vergangenheit past
vergessen (vergißt),
  vergaß, vergessen to
  forget
das Vergnügen, - pleasure,
  fun
Viel Vergnügen! Have fun!
verhaften to arrest
das Verhältnis, -se relation
verheiratet married
verkaufen to sell
der Verkaufsrekord, -e
  sales record
der Verkehrsstau, -s traffic
  jam
in einen Verkehrsstau
  geraten get into a traffic
  jam
verlangen to demand
verlassen (verläßt), verließ,
  verlassen to leave, leave
  behind
verletzt injured, hurt
verlieren, verlor, verloren
  to lose
verpassen to miss
verreist on a trip
verrückt crazy
die Verrücktheit craziness,
  madness

verschwenden to waste
Zeit verschwenden to
  waste time
sich verspäten to be late
mit Verspätung with delay
sich verstecken to hide
  (oneself)
verstehen, verstand,
  verstanden to
  understand
versuchen to try, attempt
vertragen (verträgt),
  vertrug, vertragen to
  endure, tolerate
der Vertreter, - traveling
  salesman, deputy,
  representative
der Verwandte, -n relative
verwöhnen to spoil,
  pamper
verzweifelt desperate
viel much
vielleicht perhaps
das Vitamin, -e vitamin
der Vogel, -̈ bird
das Volk, -̈er people
der Volkspolizist, -en
  people's policeman (in
  the German Democratic
  Republic)
von of, from
von ... bis from ... to
  (until)
vor in front of, before
vorbei·kommen, kam
  vorbei, ist
  vorbeigekommen to
  pass (by), to come over
vor·gehen, ging vor, ist
  vorgegangen to go
  ahead
vor·legen to put before
die Vorlesung, -en lecture
vorsichtig careful, cautious
der Vorsitzende, -n
  chairman (person)
vor·stellen to introduce
der Vorteil, -e advantage

vor·treten (tritt vor), trat vor, ist vorgetreten to step forward

das Vorurteil, -e prejudice

vor·ziehen, zog vor, vorgezogen prefer, like better

vulgär vulgar

W

der Wagen, - car

der Wagenheber, - car jack

die Wahl, -en choice, election

wählen to choose, elect

während during, while

wahrscheinlich probable, probably

der Wald, ¨-er forest

die Wand, ¨-e wall

wandern to hike

wann when

warm warm

die Wärme warmth

warten (auf + acc.) to wait (for)

warum why

was what, whatever

was für what kind of a

die Wäsche the laundry

sich waschen to wash (oneself)

das Wasser water

die Wasserpistole, -n water pistol, squirt gun

wecken to awaken

der Wecker, - alarm clock

der Weg, -e way, path

auf dem Weg on the way

weg away

weg·gehen, ging weg, ist weggegangen to go away

weg·nehmen (nimmt weg), nahm weg, weggenommen to take

away

weg·rennen, rannte weg, ist weggerannt to run away

weil because

der Wein, -e wine

weinen to cry

die Weinflasche, -n wine bottle

die Weise, -n way, method

weiß white

weit far (away)

weiter further

weiter·fahren (fährt weiter) fuhr weiter, ist weitergefahren to drive on

weiter·gehen, ging weiter, ist weitergegangen to continue on, to walk on

der Weitsprung broad jump

welch which

die Welt, -en world

weltbekannt world-renowned

weltberühmt world famous

der Weltmeister, - world champion

der Weltraum outer space

der Weltrekord, -e world record

wem (to) whom

wen whom

wenig little, not much

wenn when, if

wer who

werden (wird), wurde, ist geworden to become

werfen (wirft), warf, geworfen to throw

das Werkzeug, -e tool

der Wert, -e value, worth

das Wesen, - being, living thing

wessen whose

das Wetter weather

wichtig important

wickeln to roll (up), wrap

wie how

wie lange how long

wieviel how much

wie viele how many

wieder again

auf Wiedersehen good-bye

wiegen, wog, gewogen to weigh

die Windel, -n diaper

der Windhund, -e greyhound

winken to wave

der Winter, - winter

der Wintermantel, ¨- winter coat

wir we

wirken to take effect, work

wirklich really

der Wirt, -e host, landlord

die Wirtschaft, -en inn; economy

wissen (weiß), wußte, gewußt to know

der Witz, -e joke

wo where

die Woche, -n week

wofür for what, what for

wogegen against what

woher from where

wohin where, where to

wohl well, probably, apparently

wohnen to live, reside

die Wohnung, -en apartment, dwelling

das Wohnzimmer, - living room

die Wölfin, -nen she-wolf

der Wolkenkratzer, - skyscraper

wollen to want

womit with what

woran at what, by what

das Wort, ¨-er word

worüber about what
wovor of what, from what
wozu to what end
das Wunder, - miracle, wonder
wunderbar wonderful
wünschen to wish
die Wurst, ̈-e sausage
die Wut rage, fury
wütend furious, enraged

Z

zahlen to pay
der Zahn, ̈-e tooth
der Zahnarzt, ̈-e dentist
die Zahnpasta toothpaste
zehn ten
der Zehnkampf decathlon
das Zeichen, - sign, signal
zeigen to show
die Zeit, -en time, period
die Zeitung, -en newspaper
die Zensur, -en mark, grade; censorship
zerbrechen (zerbricht), zerbrach, ist zerbrochen to break in pieces
der Ziegenbock, ̈-e billy-goat
ziemlich considerable, fairly, rather

die Zigarette, -n cigarette
das Zimmer, - room
der Zirkus, -se circus
der Zucker sugar
zu to, towards
der Zufall, ̈-e chance, accident
zufrieden satisfied, content
der Zug, ̈-e train
zugleich at the same time
zu·hören to listen to
die Zukunft future
zu·machen to close, shut
zunächst first of all
zu·nehmen (nimmt zu), nahm zu, hat zugenommen to gain weight
zurück·geben (gibt zurück), gab zurück, zurückgegeben to give back
zurück·bekommen, bekam zurück, zurückbekommen to get back
zurück·gehen, ging zurück, zurückgegangen to go back
zurück·jagen to chase back

zurück·kehren to come back, return
zurück·kommen, kam zurück, ist zurückgekommen to come back, return
zurück·treten (tritt zurück), trat zurück, ist zurückgetreten to step back
zusammen together
zusammen·bleiben, blieb zusammen, ist zusammengeblieben to stay together
zusammen·kleben to stick, glue together
zuschauen to look at, watch
der Zuschauer, - spectator
zu·stimmen to agree to
zu·treffen (trifft zu), traf zu, zugetroffen to apply to, be true of
zwölf twelve
zuviel too much
zwei two
zweimal twice
der Zweite second
der Zwilling, -e twin
zwischen between

WÖRTERVERZEICHNIS
ENGLISCH-DEUTSCH

A

abolished beseitigt,
abgeschafft
to abstract abstrahieren
accident der Unfall, ¨-e
active aktiv
to add addieren
adventure das
Abenteuer, -
to advertise Reklame
machen (für)
advertisement die
Reklame, -n, die
Werbung
to be afraid (of) Angst
haben (vor + *Dativ*),
sich fürchten (vor +
Dativ)
age das Alter
agent der Agent, -en
to agree to zu·stimmen
(+ *Dativ*)
alarm clock der Wecker, -
alcohol der Alkohol
to be allowed to dürfen
almost fast
alone allein
along entlang *(for
instance:* den Fluß
entlang)
already schon
always immer
anarchist der Anarchist,
-en
angry böse
animal das Tier, -e
to annoy ärgern
another ein anderer, eine
andere, ein anderes;
noch einer (eine, eins)
answer die Antwort, -en
to answer beantworten,

antworten
apple der Apfel, ¨-
to apologize sich
entschuldigen
architect der Architekt,
-en
architecture die
Architektur
to arise, to get up
auf·stehen, stand auf, ist
aufgestanden
to arrange a date sich
verabreden
to arrive an·kommen, kam
an, ist angekommen
ashore an Land
to swim ashore an Land
schwimmen
to ask fragen
to ask a question eine
Frage stellen
to attack an·greifen, griff
an, angegriffen

B

baby das Baby, -s
bad schlecht
bank account das
Bankkonto, -ten
bar die Bar, -s
to bark bellen
basement der Keller, -
bathrobe der
Bademantel, ¨-
bathroom das
Badezimmer, -
to beat schlagen (schlägt),
schlug, geschlagen
beautiful schön
become werden (wird),
wurde, ist geworden
bed das Bett, -en

bedroom das
Schlafzimmer, -
beer das Bier, -e
begin beginnen, begann,
begonnen
behind hinter
belong gehören (+ *Dativ*)
bench die Bank, ¨-e
big groß
to ride a bike rad·fahren,
fuhr Rad, ist radgefahren
birthday der Geburtstag,
-e
to bite beißen, biß,
gebissen
black schwarz
blessing der Segen, -
blue blau
boat das Boot, -e
bomb die Bombe, -n
book das Buch, ¨-er
boot der Stiefel, -
boring langweilig
bottle die Flasche, -n
to box boxen
boyfriend der Freund, -e
bread das Brot, -e
to break zerbrechen
(zerbricht), zerbrach, ist
zerbrochen
breakfast das Frühstück
bride die Braut, ¨-e
bridegroom der
Bräutigam, -e
to bring bringen, brachte,
gebracht
broken zerbrochen, kaputt
brother der Bruder, ¨-
brother-in-law der
Schwager, ¨-
to brush one's teeth sich
die Zähne putzen
to build bauen

building material das Baumaterial, -ien
building permit die Baugenehmigung, -en
building site der Bauplatz, -̈e
bunny das Häschen, -
bus der Bus, -se
business das Geschäft, -e
to buy kaufen

C

cake der Kuchen, -
to call rufen, rief, gerufen
to call on the phone an·rufen, rief an, angerufen
camera die Kamera, -s
can, to be able to können
cap die Mütze, -n
capitalist der Kapitalist, -en
to capsize kentern
captain der Kapitän, -e (*ship*) der Hauptmann, die Hauptleute (*military*)
car das Auto, -s, der Wagen, -
to play cards Karten spielen
carpet der Teppich, -e
to carry tragen (trägt), trug, getragen
to carry away weg·tragen, trug weg, weggetragen
cat die Katze, -n
to catch fangen (fängt), fing, gefangen
ceremony die Zeremonie, -n
chain reaction die Kettenreaktion, -en
chairman der (die) Vorsitzende, -n
chamber of commerce die Handelskammer, -n
chance die Chance, -n

to change (clothes) sich um·ziehen, zog um, umgezogen
chauvinist der Chauvinist, -en
cheap billig
to cheat betrügen
to check nach·sehen, (sieht nach), sah nach, nachgesehen; prüfen
chemical industry die chemische Industrie
to chew kauen
child das Kind, -er
children's room das Kinderzimmer, -
to choose wählen
church choir der Kirchenchor, -̈e
cigarette die Zigarette, -n
city die Stadt, -̈e
city planning die Stadtplanung, -en
to clean reinigen
to clean up auf·räumen
clean rein, sauber
clever klug
climate das Klima
to close zu·machen
cloud die Wolke, -n
club der Klub, -s
coast die Küste, -n
coat der Mantel, -̈
coffee der Kaffee
cold kalt
to comb (one's hair) (sich) kämmen
to come kommen, kam, ist gekommen
to come here her·kommen, kam her, ist hergekommen
to come home nach Hause kommen, kam nach Hause, ist nach Hause gekommen
communist der Kommunist, -en

to compensate kompensieren
competition die Konkurrenz, -en
concert das Konzert, -e
concrete der Beton
conscience das Gewissen
conservative konservativ
continue (doing something) weiter-
to copy kopieren
to cost kosten
to count zählen
to count again nach·zählen
country das Land, -̈er
crazy verrückt
crime das Verbrechen, -
to cry weinen
curious neugierig
curse der Fluch, -̈e
customer der Kunde, -n

D

to dance tanzen
to continue dancing weiter·tanzen
dangerous gefährlich
dark dunkel
daughter die Tochter, -̈
day der Tag, -e
to decide (sich) entscheiden, entschied, entschieden; (sich) entschließen, entschloß, entschlossen
to defeat besiegen
to delegate delegieren
it depends es kommt darauf an
to destroy zerstören
to die sterben (stirbt), starb, ist gestorben
different verschieden
dinner das Abendbrot, das Abendessen, -
dirty schmutzig

disappointment die Enttäuschung, -en
to discover entdecken
to discuss diskutieren
to divide dividieren
doctor der Arzt, ̈-e; die Ärztin, -nen
dog der Hund, -e
door die Tür, -en
double doppelt
to dress an·ziehen, zog an, angezogen
to dress oneself sich an·ziehen, sich (an)·kleiden
a drink das (alkoholische) Getränk, -e
to drink trinken, trank, getrunken
to drive fahren (fährt), fuhr, ist gefahren
to drive off ab·fahren (fährt ab), fuhr ab, ist abgefahren
to drive there hin·fahren, (fährt hin), fuhr hin, ist hingefahren
drunk betrunken
dumb dumm

E

early früh
to eat essen (ißt), aß, gegessen
to eat up auf·essen (ißt auf), aß auf, hat aufgegessen
economy die Wirtschaft, -en
eerie unheimlich
elegant elegant
to eliminate eliminieren
emancipated emanzipiert
to embrace umarmen
enough genug
et cetera und so weiter, u.s.w.

every jeder, jede, jedes
everybody jeder, jede, jedes
to set a bad example ein schlechtes Beispiel geben
exciting aufregend
to expect erwarten
expensive teuer
to exploit ausbeuten
to export exportieren

F

to faint ohnmächtig werden
faithful treu
family die Familie, -n
famous berühmt
far weit
farm der Bauernhof, ̈-e
father der Vater, ̈-
to feed füttern
fast schnell
to fight kämpfen
film der Film, -e
film director der Filmdirektor, -en
filmstar der Filmstar, -s
to find finden, fand, gefunden
to fit in passen zu
to flirt flirten
floor (level in a house) das Stockwerk, -e, der Stock, ̈-e
to fly fliegen, flog, ist geflogen
fish der Fisch, -e
to fish fischen, angeln
to flow fließen, floß, ist geflossen
flower die Blume, -n
forest der Wald, ̈-er
free kostenlos, frei
freedom die Freiheit
freighter der Frachter, -
fresh frisch

friend der Freund, -e, die Freundin, -nen
friendly freundlich
in front of vor
frustrated frustriert

G

to gain weight zu·nehmen (nimmt zu), nahm zu, zugenommen
to buy gas tanken
gasoline das Benzin
gentleman der Herr, -en
to get (fetch) holen
to get in ein·steigen, stieg ein, ist eingestiegen
to get out aus·steigen, stieg aus, ist ausgestiegen
to get up auf·stehen, stand auf, ist aufgestanden
girl das Mädchen, -
girlfriend die Freundin, -nen
to give geben (gibt), gab, gegeben
to give back zurück·geben (gibt zurück), gab zurück, hat zurückgegeben
glass das Glas, ̈-er
to go gehen, ging, ist gegangen
to go ahead, go to the front vor·gehen, ging vor, ist vorgegangen
to go away fort·gehen, ging fort, ist fortgegangen
to go and eat essen·gehen, ging essen, ist essengegangen
to go for a walk spazieren·gehen, ging spazieren, ist spazierengegangen
to go home nach Hause

gehen, ging nach Hause, ist nach Hause gegangen

to go out aus·gehen, ging aus, ist ausgegangen

to go to the movies ins Kino gehen, ging ins Kino, ist ins Kino gegangen

good gut

good-for-nothing der Tunichtgut, -e

government die Regierung, -en

grandchild das Enkelkind, -er

great groß

grey grau

guest der Gast, -̈e

H

haircut der Haarschnitt, -e

to happen passieren; geschehen, (geschieht) geschah, ist geschehen

harmless unschädlich

to hate hassen

to have haben (hat), hatte, gehabt

head der Kopf, -̈e

headache das Kopweh, Kopfschmerzen (pl.)

healthy gesund

helicopter der Hubschrauber, -

to say hello guten Tag sagen

to help helfen (hilft), half, geholfen

here hier

to hide (sich) verstecken; (sich) verbergen (verbirgt), verbarg, verborgen

to hit schlagen (schlägt), schlug, geschlagen

to hold halten (hält), hielt, gehalten

home die Heimat, das Zuhause

homework die Hausaufgabe, -n

to honk hupen

hotel das Hotel, -s

house das Haus, -̈er

at home zu Hause

house number die Hausnummer, -n

how wie

How are you? Wie geht es Ihnen?

humor der Humor

hungry hungrig

to be hungry hungrig sein; Hunger haben

husband der Mann, -̈er, der Ehemann, -̈er

I

ice-cream das Eis, die Eiskrem

idea die Idee, -n

to have no idea keine Ahnung haben

to idealize idealisieren

to identify identifizieren

idiot der Idiot, -en

if wenn; ob

to ignore ignorieren, nicht beachten

ill krank

to import importieren

to improvise improvisieren

source of income die Einnahmequelle, -n

to inform informieren

instrument das Instrument, -e

intelligent intelligent

interesting interessant

interview das Interview, -s

to invite ein·laden (lädt ein), lud ein, eingeladen

to irritate irritieren, ärgern

K

to kill töten

to jump springen, sprang, ist gesprungen

king der König, -e

kitchen die Küche, -n

to kneel knien

to get to know, become acquainted kennen·lernen

to know by heart auswendig kennen, kannte, gekannt

L

land das Land, -̈er

language die Sprache, -n

late spät, zu spät

to come late zu spät kommen, kam zu spät, ist zu spät gekommen

lawyer der Rechtsanwalt, -̈e

to learn lernen

to leave verlassen (verläßt), verließ, verlassen

leftover der Rest, -e

leg das Bein, -e

length die Länge, -n

letter der Brief, -e

license plate das Nummernschild, -er

to lie (repose) liegen, lag, gelegen

lie die Lüge, -n

to lie lügen, log, gelogen

to lie down sich hin·legen

life vest die Schwimmweste, -n

light das Licht, -er

like to (+ _verb_) gern

to like gern haben, mögen

lion der Löwe, -n

to listen to hören

to live leben; wohnen

living room das

Wohnzimmer, -
local (regional) poet der Heimatdichter, -
lonely einsam
long lang
how long (*temporal*) wie lange
so long so lange
to look at an·sehen (sieht an), sah an, angesehen
to look forward to sich freuen auf (+ *Akkusativ*)
to look out auf·passen
a lot viel
to love lieben
love story der Liebesroman, -e
luck das Glück

M

mad verrückt
to make machen
man der Mann, -̈er
to march marschieren
to marinate marinieren
married verheiratet
to marry heiraten
matter die Sache, -n, die Angelegenheit, -en
may dürfen
maybe vielleicht
mayor der Bürgermeister, -
to mean bedeuten, meinen
to meet (sich) treffen (trifft), traf, getroffen
to memorize auswendig lernen
mild mild
milk die Milch
minute die Minute, -n
money das Geld
moon der Mond, -e
moonshine bar die Mondscheinbar, -s
morals die Moral
more mehr
morning der Morgen, -

this morning heute morgen
most of all am liebsten
mother die Mutter, -̈
motorcycle das Motorrad, -̈er
mountain der Berg, -e
mouse die Maus, -̈e
movie der Film, -e
much viel
too much zuviel
to multiply multiplizieren
music die Musik
must, to have to müssen

N

to navigate navigieren
to need brauchen
neighbor der Nachbar, -n
nervous nervös
never nie
new neu
newspaper die Zeitung, -en
noise der Lärm
none keiner, keine, keines
nosy neugierig
not a, not any kein, keine, kein, keine (pl.)
to notice merken, bemerken
nuclear Kern-, Atom-
number die Zahl, -en

O

ocean das Meer, -e, der Ozean, -e
offended beleidigt
often oft
oil industry die Ölindustrie, -n
old alt
one (you, people, they) man
one another einander
only nur

to open auf·machen
to order bestellen
ought to, should sollen
overcast trüb, bedeckt
owner der Besitzer, -

P

pacifist der Pazifist, -en
pants die Hose, -n
parents die Eltern (*pl.*)
park der Park, -s
to park parken
parking lot der Parkplatz, -̈e
partner der Partner, -, die Partnerin, -nen
pastor der Pastor, -en
to pay bezahlen
people die Leute (*pl.*)
person die Person, -en
pet das Haustier, -e
to pet streicheln
phone das Telephon, -e
to phone telephonieren
phone number die Telephonnummer, -n
to photograph photographieren
to pick up auf·heben, hob auf, aufgehoben (in the sense of: lift from the ground or keep)
ab·holen (in the sense of: picking up somebody who is waiting for you or something that is kept for you)
plane das Flugzeug, -e
play (drama) das Theaterstück, -e
to play spielen
to play cards Karten spielen
poem das Gedicht, -e
police die Polizei
policeman der Polizist, -en
poor arm

practical praktisch
to praise loben
to pray beten
prayer das Gebet, -e
to prefer lieber haben,
vor·ziehen, zog vor,
vorgezogen
president der Präsident,
-en
priest der Priester, -
privacy das Privatleben
that is a private matter
das ist Privatsache
problem das Problem, -e
to produce produzieren
to program
programmieren
to protest protestieren
proverb das Sprichwort,
-er
public das Publikum,
öffentlich
to put before vor·legen
to qualify qualifizieren

Q

queen die Königin, -nen
question die Frage, -n
to ask a question eine
Frage stellen

R

radio das Radio, -s
rain der Regen
to rain regnen
raincoat der Regenmantel,
-
to ratify ratifizieren
to read lesen (liest), las,
gelesen
really wirklich
to recommend empfehlen
(empfiehlt), empfahl,
empfohlen
record die Platte, -n
record player der

Plattenspieler, -
refrigerator der
Kühlschrank, -e
relationship das
Verhältnis, -se, die
Beziehung, -en
relative der Verwandte, -n
to relax sich entspannen
to repair reparieren
to repeat wiederholen
reporter der Reporter, -
to respect respektieren
restaurant das Restaurant,
-s
revolution die Revolution,
-en
rich reich
to ride (a horse) reiten,
ritt, geritten
ridiculous lächerlich
to ring klingeln
ring der Ring, -e
river der Fluß, -sse
rocket die Rakete, -n
to run laufen (läuft), lief,
ist gelaufen
to run away weg·laufen
(läuft weg), lief weg, ist
weggelaufen
Russia Rußland

S

to save (money) sparen
to save (rescue) retten
to say sagen
school die Schule, -n
to see sehen (sieht), sah,
gesehen
to sell verkaufen
semi-nude halbnackt
to send senden, schicken
sentimental sentimental
service die Bedienung
seven sieben
to shave (sich) rasieren
shirt das Hemd, -en
shoe der Schuh, -e

to go shopping einkaufen
gehen, ging einkaufen,
ist einkaufen gegangen
shore das Ufer, -
short kurz
should sollen
to shout schreien, schrie,
geschrien
to show zeigen
to shower (sich) duschen
sick krank
sin die Sünde, -n
to sing singen, sang,
gesungen
to sink sinken, sank, ist
gesunken
to sit sitzen, saß, gesessen
sketch die Skizze, -n
to ski skilaufen (läuft Ski),
lief Ski, ist skigelaufen
skyscraper der
Wolkenkratzer, -
to sled Schlitten fahren
(fährt Schlitten), fuhr
Schlitten, ist Schlitten
gefahren
to sleep schlafen (schläft),
schlief, geschlafen
to sleep late aus·schlafen
to go to bed (sleep)
schlafen gehen, ins Bett
gehen, ging schlafen (ins
Bett), ist schlafen (ins
Bett) gegangen
small klein
to smile lächeln
smog der Smog
to smoke rauchen
soap die Seife, -n
soccer, soccer ball der
Fußball, -e
sofa das Sofa, -s
to solve lösen
something etwas
son der Sohn, -e
song das Lied, -er
soul die Seele, -n
to speak sprechen

(spricht), sprach, gesprochen
spectator der Zuschauer, -
to give a speech eine Rede halten (hält), hielt, gehalten
to spoil verwöhnen
sport der Sport
to squirt spritzen
stairs die Treppe, -n
to come down the stairs die Treppe herunter·kommen, kam herunter, ist heruntergekommen
to stand stehen, stand, gestanden
stairway die Treppe, -n
to stay bleiben, blieb, ist geblieben
to stay together zusammen·bleiben
to stay up late lange auf·bleiben
to steal stehlen (stiehlt), stahl, gestohlen
step der Schritt, -e
to step forward vortreten, tritt vor, trat vor, ist vorgetreten
to stick together zusammen·kleben
to stop (an)·halten, (hält), hielt, gehalten
store das Geschäft, -e der Laden, -
street die Straße, -n
strong stark
student der Student, -en die Studentin, -nen
studies das Studium, -dien
to study studieren
stupid dumm
style der Stil, -e
suit der Anzug, -e
sun die Sonne, -n
supermarket der Supermarkt, -e

to be supposed to sollen
to survive überleben
to swear (an oath) schwören, schwor, geschworen
to swear (in the sense of curse) fluchen
to swim schwimmen, schwamm, ist geschwommen
to go swimming schwimmen gehen, ging schwimmen, ist schwimmen gegangen
swimsuit der Badeanzug, -e
to switch off ab·schalten
to switch on an·schalten

T

to take nehmen (nimmt), nahm, genommen
to take along mit·nehmen, (nimmt mit), nahm mit, mitgenommen
to take away weg·nehmen (nimmt weg), nahm weg, weggenommen
to talk sprechen (spricht), sprach, gesprochen
tall groß
taste der Geschmack, -er
to taste schmecken
to taste (in the sense of: trying something) probieren
taxes Steuern (pl.)
tea der Tee
teacher der Lehrer, -
telegram das Telegramm, -e
to telegraph telegraphieren
to telephone telephonieren
television das Fernsehen
to watch television

fernsehen (sieht fern), sah fern, hat ferngesehen
to tell sagen, erzählen
tennis Tennis
to test testen, prüfen
test der Test, -s, die Prüfung, -en
theater das Theater, -
there is (are) es gibt
to think denken, dachte, gedacht
thirsty durstig
to threaten drohen
to throw werfen (wirft), warf, geworfen
tight eng
time die Zeit, -en
tired müde
today heute
tomorrow morgen
too auch
tool das Werkzeug, -e
traffic jam der Verkehrsstau, -s
train der Zug, -e
to travel reisen
tree der Baum, -e
trip die Reise, -n
trunk der Stamm, -e
truth die Wahrheit
to try versuchen, probieren
to turn on an·drehen, an·schalten
twice zweimal
two zwei
to type tippen
type der Typ, -en

U

ugly häßlich
umbrella der Regenschirm, -e
uncle der Onkel, -
under unter
to understand verstehen, verstand, verstanden

unemployment die Arbeitslosigkeit
unhappy unglücklich
United States die Vereinigten Staaten
unusual ungewöhnlich
useful nützlich

V

vacation (die) Ferien (*pl.*)
to go on vacation in Urlaub fahren (fährt in Urlaub) fuhr in Urlaub, ist in Urlaub gefahren
to ventilate ventilieren
to verify verifizieren
very sehr
visible sichtbar
to visit besuchen
to vote wählen
vulnerable verwundbar

W

to wait (for) warten (auf + *Akkusativ*)
to walk gehen, ging, ist gegangen, zu Fuß gehen
to take a walk spazierengehen, ging spazieren, ist spazierengegangen
to want to wollen
warm warm
wash die Wäsche
to wash waschen, sich waschen
to waste verschwenden
to watch beobachten, auf·passen
water pistol die Wasserpistole, -n
to waterski Wasserski laufen (fahren)
weak schwach
to wear tragen (trägt), trug, getragen
weather das Wetter
week die Woche, -n
weekend das Wochenende, -n
well gut, wohl
west der Western, West-
wet naß

when wann, als
where wo
why warum
wife die Frau, -en, die Ehefrau, -en
will, shall werden (wird)
window das Fenster, -
wine der Wein, -e
wine bottle die Weinflasche, -n
winter der Winter, -
with mit
without ohne
woman die Frau, -en
word das Wort, ¨-er
to have the last word das letzte Wort haben
work, job die Arbeit, -en
to work arbeiten
to write schreiben, schrieb, geschrieben

Y

yard der Hof, ¨-e
young jung